Responsible Management Education

Responsible Management Education

Some Voices From Asia

Edited by
Ranjini Swamy

BEP BUSINESS EXPERT PRESS

Responsible Management Education: Some Voices From Asia

First published in 2017 by
Business Expert Press, LLC
222 East 46th Street, New York, NY 10017
www.businessexpertpress.com

ISBN-13: 978-1-63157-682-9 (paperback)
ISBN-13: 978-1-63157-683-6 (e-book)

Business Expert Press Principles for Responsible Management Education Collection

Collection ISSN: 2331-0014 (print)
Collection ISSN: 2331-0022 (electronic)

Cover and interior design by Exeter Premedia Services Private Ltd., Chennai, India

First edition: 2017

10 9 8 7 6 5 4 3 2 1

Printed in the United States of America.

Abstract

Asia is home to a very large number of business schools. This edited collection emerged from the need to know about how business schools in Asia are inculcating Responsible Management. The book describes how some Asian business schools are incorporating ethics, social responsibility, and sustainability into their curricular and extra-curricular activities. It identifies the challenges faced in providing such education and the implications thereof. In the process it captures the unique flavor of Asian business schools.

Data for the book was sourced from the workshop proceedings of the 6th PRME Asia Forum held in Goa, India in November 2015 and from case studies submitted before the Forum. The Workshop sessions were a demonstration-cum-discussion about the design and conduct of some courses on responsible management. The sessions were led by faculty members from (a) public autonomous institutes such as the Indian Institute of Management, Ahmedabad; (b) private autonomous institutes such as XLRI, Jamshedpur and MDI, Gurgaon; and (c) university departments such as The School of Economics and Management at Tsinghua University in China.

Some of the case studies detail the curricular interventions introduced by some business schools to inculcate responsible management. Others share the experiences of faculty members in designing and conducting specific courses/modules on responsible management, the challenges experienced in inculcating responsible management and responses. The authors are faculty members/administrators representing the Indira School of Business Studies, Pune, India; the Hang Seng Management College, Hong Kong; the Colegio de San Juan de Letran Calamba, Philippines; the Indian Institute of Management, Indore, India; the KIIT School of Rural Management, Orissa, India; and the Department of Management Studies at a University in western India.

Together the workshop proceedings and the case studies suggest that the sampled Asian business schools have introduced courses/modules on responsible management. However, few appear to have made responsible management a central part of business school strategy. There is need to develop a different worldview of education, one that focuses on the wellbeing of the planet and people, rather than the wellbeing of business alone. Support from other stakeholders is critical for this to occur. Additionally, faculty members require training and encouragement to integrate responsible management in their research agendas and courses.

Keywords

Asian business schools, Ethics, Responsible Management, Responsible Management Education, Sustainability

Contents

Introduction

The South Asian Context

In the last decade, Asian economies have been growing rapidly, riding on globalization, new technology, and market-oriented reforms. Unfettered economic growth has been accompanied by several social and environmental challenges. First, rapid economic growth has been accompanied by higher exploitation of natural resources and higher amount of wastes. These have adversely affected the livelihood and identities of several local communities and threatened the survival of several species that could be integral to the sustenance of the planet.[1] Second, the benefits of economic growth in Asia are not reaching all sections as is evident in the lower per capita gross domestic product (GDP)[2] of these economies relative to developed economies. The result is wasted human capital, increased social tension, and increased pressure for populist policies.

South Asia for instance, has grown at 6 to 9 percent per year in the period 2010 to 2015 but its per capita income during that period has been $692, the lowest among all regions. The benefits of such a model of economic development has reached the owners of capital and the more educated, city-based sections of the Asian population.[3] The costs have been borne by the less-educated, rural-based population in the region. The region is home to 22 percent of the world's population but 44 percent of the world's poor. Recent trends indicate that inequality of income and opportunity has worsened with rapid growth.[4] For instance, school-age children from the poorest income quintile are five times more likely to be

---

[1] Ibid.

[2] Quah, E. 2015. "Pursuing Economic Growth in Asia: the Environmental Challenge." *The World Economy* 38, no. 10, pp. 1487–504.

[3] Source: www.oecd.org/social/asia-challenges.htm (accessed March 10, 2017).

[4] Source: www.riport.org/wp-content/uploads/pdf%20downloads/publications/Mellinium%20Development%20goals.pdf (accessed March 10, 2017).

out of school than children of the richest quintile. This section of the society is therefore likely to have limited access to livelihood opportunities.

Responsible Management and Leadership

Business has been the engine of technological and economic growth in Asia but is also contributing to the region's social and environmental challenges. As a result, several sections of society have become more critical of business and are demanding a new social contract.[5] Society expects business to help realize an inclusive, sustainable society through their corporate social responsibility (CSR) investments and by practicing responsible management and leadership. These expectations are expressed through the social media, government regulations, and representations of the civil society. When these expectations are not met, business has had to face losses. As a result, some Asian businesses are beginning to adopt a wider definition of their responsibility toward society.[6]

There is no accepted definition of the terms "responsible management" and "responsible leadership." However, a number of criteria could be incorporated in the definition set of responsible management such as the "development of moral values, soft skills, systemic thinking, and a shared vision that is respectful, participative and inclusive."[7] Responsible leadership is to consider, act in accordance with, and respond to the needs of a broader set of global and local stakeholders, with the aim of ensuring legitimacy of the organization and developing a symbiotic relation with stakeholders.[8]

---

[5] Smit, A. 2013. "Responsible Leadership Development Through Management Education: A Business Ethics Perspective." *African Journal of Business Ethics* 7, no. 2, Conference Edition.

[6] Jose, P. D. 2016. "Sustainability Education in Indian Business Schools: a Status Review." AD-minister [S.l.], n. 28, pp. 255–272. ISSN 2256-4322. Available at: http://publicaciones.eafit.edu.co/index.php/administer/article/view/3575/3005 (accessed March 11, 2017). doi: http://dx.doi.org/10.17230/ad-minister.28.13

[7] Nonet, G., K. Kussel, and L. Meijs. 2016. "Understanding Responsible Management: Emerging Themes and Variations from European Business School Programs." *Journal of Business Ethics* 139, pp. 717–36.

[8] Doh, J.P., and N.R. Quigley. 2014. "Responsible Leadership and Stakeholder Management: Influence Pathways and Organizational Outcomes." *Academy of Management Perspectives* 28, no. 3, pp. 255–274.

Responsible leadership could include "standing up for what one believes is right. ... value-based and moral decision-making, sharing ideals of societal well-being and a sense of accountability (responsiveness) and stakeholder-orientation."[9] The United Nations (UN) Global Compact has emphasized responsible management and leadership in the areas of human rights (including the rights of indigenous people affected by business decisions), labor standards, environment, and anticorruption.

The practice of responsible management and leadership requires traditional managerial functions—planning, organizing, leading, and controlling—to be discharged differently. The planning function must focus on designing organizations for sustainability in the markets and *in society* and designing new technologies, products/services that address social and environmental challenges. The organizing function needs to focus on operationalizing strategies in a manner that includes the concerns of *all stakeholders* in the supply chain. Leading (especially by the human resource professionals) requires developing a communication strategy that ensures continued goodwill of the employees and the local community. Controlling requires the development of measures that ensure continued *accountability to all stakeholders*, not just shareholders.[10]

To achieve this, managers and leaders need to understand the mutually reinforcing nature of relationships among business, society, and the ecological environment. They must be able to integrate traditional economic considerations with ethical, social, and environmental considerations while formulating and implementing business strategies and making decisions.[11] Importantly, they need to understand, be open to, and synthesize the diverse perspectives of various stakeholders while formulating and implementing business strategies.

---

[9] Ibid.

[10] Lenn, D. J. 2015. "Principles of Responsible Management: Global Sustainability, Responsibility and Ethics." *Academy of Management Learning and Education* 14, no. 2, pp. 299–301.

[11] Carroll, A., and A. Buchholtz. 2008. "Business and Society: Ethics and Stakeholder Management." Cengage Learning. In Smit, A. 2013. "Responsible Leadership Development Through Management Education: A Business Ethics Perspective." *African Journal of Business Ethics* 7, no. 2, Conference Edition.

The role of business schools in developing such managers and leaders is evident. In 2002, the UN General Assembly announced 2005 to 2014 as the decade of Education for Sustainable Development. Education was seen not just as a fundamental right but as an important instrument to help inculcate the values, attitudes, and lifestyle that would ensure an inclusive, sustainable society. This could require formulating a set of principles to guide all the academic and administrative activities of business schools, facilitating networks among stakeholders and fostering supportive research, teaching, action, and governance.[12]

In 2007, on the recommendation of academic stakeholders of the UN Global Compact, "a principle-based global engagement platform" called the Principles for Responsible Management Education (PRME) was created to promote responsible management education across the world. The six principles underlying such a platform—Purpose, Values, Method Research, Partnership, and Dialogue—could act as guidelines for integrating responsible management education in all academic activities.[13] The principles do not define responsible management education, preferring instead that business schools evolve such definitions.

Responsible Management Education

Business school education is presently informed by a variety of competing, even contradictory paradigms. However, at a broad level, the education shares the following assumptions: Business is a dominant part of society and needs to be treated as such. The purpose of business is growth and maximization of shareholder value. Other purposes are either incidental or to be ignored. Business strategies and decisions should help achieve the purpose. They must be made/reviewed by focusing on the measurable, calculable costs and benefits to business. As the ethical or moral implications of business decisions are intangible, they are not so

---

[12] Alcarez, J. M., and T. Eappen. 2010. "An Interview with Manuel Escudero. The United Nations' Principles for Responsible Management Education: a global call for Sustainability." *Academy of Management Learning & Education* 9, no. 3, pp. 542–550.

[13] Source: http://unprme.org/about-prme/the-six-principles.php

significant. While formulating and implementing strategies, it is important to "control" those stakeholders who are instrumental to achievement
of the business purpose. These stakeholders are rational, self-interest
maximizers. To control their behavior, it is necessary to align the reward
systems with their self-interest. Any decision or action is only justified if
it benefits business.

As a result of these widely held assumptions, managers are often
ill prepared to perceive the potential human and environmental
consequences of their decisions. Take the case of Foxconn, China's largest
employer and a dominant manufacturer for companies like Dell and
Apple. In 2012, there were media reports of suicides and labor unrest at
its plants in China. The Fair Labor Association investigated the issue and
found lapses in the working conditions that could explain these suicides
and the labor unrest. The Chairman of the company admitted that he had
failed to see the significance of worker suicides early enough.[14]

To promote a greater sensitivity to the human and environmental
implications of managerial decisions, a shift towards human- and planet-
centered paradigm of management appears necessary. This would require
new competencies.[15] It would also require a pedagogy that exposes students to the tensions between business and society so that students are
better prepared to make judgments in complex situations.[16] Faculty
members need to emphasize more active—rather than passive—learning.
They could tap into the experiences of students on live projects or sim-
ulations to bring home the interdependence between business and society and illustrate the complexities of responsible decision-making. They
could help students interact with representatives of various stakeholders
(instrumental or not-so instrumental to business) to understand differing
values and perspectives. They could adopt the Socratic mode to promote

---

[14] Abueg, L.C., M.M.R. Sauler, and B. Teehankee. 2014. "Toward a Common Good Model
of the Firm." *DLSU Business and Economics Review* 24, no. 1, pp. 1–12.

[15] Kelley, S., and R. Nahser. 2014. "Developing Sustainable Strategies: Foundations,
Method and Pedagogy." *Journal of Business Ethics* 123, pp. 631–644.

[16] Fougere, M., N. Solitander, and S. Young. 2014. "Exploring and Exposing Values in
Management Education: Problematizing Final Vocabularies in Order to Enhance Moral
Imagination." *Journal of Business Ethics* 120, pp. 175–187.

reflection among students about their mind-sets (by asking questions such as "so what? who cares?").[17]

Such a transformative change in business school curriculum could be challenging. Four approaches could be adopted to integrate responsible management education into the curriculum:

(a) Integrate *into an existing discipline-based course* through use of case studies/visiting lectures or presentations or by introducing additional topics relating to responsible management and sustainability. This could be viewed as the first step toward integrating sustainability. It is also the easiest to implement as it does not require much review.

(b) Create *new stand-alone courses within a discipline.* This option allows a deeper relation between responsible management, sustainability and the specific discipline. However, it could isolate responsible management and sustainability by associating them too narrowly with a discipline.

(c) Integrate into existing common core courses across disciplines. This option allows integration of responsible management and sustainability across the *core courses of all disciplines* and therefore ensures sustained exposure to entire batches of students. However, it requires school-wide commitment of energy and resources.

(d) *Create new cross-disciplinary courses and programs.* This option is useful if responsible management and sustainability are part of the core strategy of the institution. It enables integration through newer, cross-disciplinary courses or programs. However, it could require maximum institute-wide support in terms of time and resources.[18]

Global Trends in Responsible Management Education

Business schools have taken small steps toward integrating responsible management and leadership into the curriculum. Students in the top 30

---

[17] Ibid.

[18] Rusinko, C. A. 2010. "Integrating Sustainability in Management and Business Education: A Matrix Approach." *Academy of Management Learning and Education* 9, no. 3, pp. 507–519

business schools are being exposed to social and environmental issues in about 25 percent of their coursework, compared to other business schools where students are exposed to such issues in just 8 percent of their coursework.[19] Many business schools have enhanced students' awareness about environmental, ethical, and social issues. However, inculcating systemic thinking, synthesis, soft skills and empathy remain a challenge for a variety of reasons. For instance, systemic thinking is constrained by a functional mind-set that is reinforced by recruiters' hiring practices and the school's resource allocation norms. Thus students are not equipped with the competencies required to be responsible managers and leaders.[20]

A study of the self-reports of PRME signatories from two dominant regions, Europe and North America, suggests that business schools in the United States report more progress in incorporating sustainability and responsibility into their academic activities. They have introduced new teaching methods, brought in guest speakers, added site visits, introduced new courses on responsible management, and modified existing courses to include a discussion on responsible management. They are more likely to have introduced a research center to conduct research on sustainability and societal issues, and to have established partnerships with nongovernmental organizations (NGOs) and the business sector.

European business schools report more progress in developing the capabilities of students to be responsible managers and leaders.[21] Earlier surveys across several business schools in Europe suggested the peripheral status of responsible management education. They have now introduced more courses on responsible management and also some interdisciplinary programs. They have also introduced responsible campus management practices. There is a felt need for alternate pedagogical approaches to teach

---

[19] Bridges, C. M., and W. B. Wilhelm. 2008. "Going Beyond Green: The 'Why and How' of Integrating Sustainability Into the Marketing Curriculum." *Journal of Marketing Education* 30, no. 1, pp. 33–46.

[20] Navarro, P. 2008. "The MBA Core Curricula of Top-Ranked US Business Schools: A Study in Failure?" *Academy of Management Learning & Education* 7, no. 1, pp. 108–123.

[21] Arac, S. K., and C. Madran. 2014. "Business School as Initiator of the Transformation to Sustainability: A Content Analysis for Business Schools in PRME." *Social Business* 4, no. 2, pp. 61–70.

responsible management. Greater integration of responsible management into research and teaching appears to be constrained by the present system of incentives.[22]

In India, responsible management education began in the early 1990s when some well-known business schools began offering electives on Environment Management. In 2012, a survey of 107 Indian business schools found that courses on Ethics were offered by almost 65 percent of the respondent schools while courses on Corporate Governance were offered by about 31 percent of them. Courses on Environment and CSR were offered by less than 15 percent of the respondents. It appears that responsible management and sustainability are commonly taught through stand-alone elective or core courses. The theme is not integrated across functional areas. Only two institutions offer new programs on Sustainable Management.[23]

Several challenges appear to deter the integration of responsible management and leadership into the business school curriculum. At a fundamental level, business schools across the world are yet to shift towards a human- and planet-centered paradigm of management.[24] In India, such a shift is constrained by the following factors: (a) the autonomous nature of business schools and the lack of collaboration with other disciplines; (b) the functional mind-set among administrators, students, and faculty members[25]; (c) the lack of faculty expertise in responsible management and sustainability; (d) nonavailability of context-specific, comprehensive

---

[22] Painter-Morland, M., E. Sabet, P. Moltan-Hill, H. Goworek, and S. Leeuw. 2016. "Beyond the Curriculum: Integrating Sustainability into Business Schools." *Journal of Business Ethics* 139, no. 4, pp. 737–754.

[23] Jose, P.D. 2016. "Sustainability Education in Indian Business Schools: a Status Review." AD-minister [S.l.], no. 28, pp. 255–272. ISSN 2256-4322. Available at: http://publicaciones.eafit.edu.co/index.php/administer/article/view/3575/3005 (accessed March 11, 2017). doi:http://dx.doi.org/10.17230/ad-minister.28.13

[24] Giacalone, R. A., and K. R. Thompson. 2008. "Business Ethics and Social Responsibility Education: A Shifting Worldview." *Academy of Management Learning & Education* 5, no. 3, pp. 266–277.

[25] Navarro, P. 2008. "The MBA Core Curricula of Top-Ranked US Business Schools: A Study in Failure?" *Academy of Management Learning & Education* 7, no. 1, pp. 108–123.

case studies/learning materials; (e) the lack of recruiter interest in responsible management or its related competencies.[26]

Survey research conducted in India provides a broad overview of the status of responsible management education in India. It would be interesting to examine whether there have been newer developments (since the survey) in the approach to inculcating responsible management. A more in-depth exploration of coursework and the curriculum adopted by some business schools could be a rich source of ideas and information in this regard. The following examples from other countries are illustrative of these benefits:

A Finnish business school has introduced a "Corporate Responsibility" Minor at the undergraduate and postgraduate levels. This includes a set of courses such as Corporate Law, Management and Organization, Marketing, Politics and Business, Supply Chain Management, and Corporate Geography. The courses discuss the relation between business and society from differing perspectives. An Australian business school has introduced a professional part-time graduate certification in Corporate Responsibility, using a multi-disciplinary perspective. The school partners with business establishments to conduct workshops where students have opportunities to engage with business. In its post graduate program in management , the school offers Responsible Management modules in all functional courses. It also offers stand-alone courses on Ethics, Business and Society, and Responsible Leadership.

Importantly, both the programs discuss the mainstream vocabulary typical of business schools—such as "shareholder centrality" and "competition"—and then juxtapose alternate vocabulary such as "development" or "caring/collaboration." Students discuss the new vocabulary and explore their implications for the corporate visions, strategies, performance objectives, and decisions. Faculty members

---

[26] Jose, P. D. 2016. "Sustainability Education in Indian Business Schools: a Status Review." AD-minister [S.l.], n. 28, pp. 255–272. ISSN 2256-4322. available at http://publicaciones.eafit.edu.co/index.php/administer/article/view/3575/3005 (accessed March 11, 2017). doi:http://dx.doi.org/10.17230/ad-minister.28.13

use active pedagogies such as research projects and case studies to promote new perspectives about the relation between business and society.[27]

Again, ESADE business school and Boston College have introduced programs in partnership with business leaders, to achieve the following purpose: (a) expose participants (usually managers, administrators, NGO employees, MBA students) to the significant challenges facing society; (b) help participants develop visions and become leaders of change for the common good. Both programs use experiential, reflective, interactive, and action-learning pedagogies to inculcate systems thinking and other related competencies. Sessions are scheduled over the weekends for approximately a year. Assignments require application of learnings at the workplace and reflection on such experiences. Alumni, business partners, and faculty members act as mentors to the participants.[28]

Detailed case studies on responsible management initiatives could provide useful ideas for those planning to inculcate responsible management. Presently there are few such case studies available, especially in the Asian context. As Asia is home to several thousand business schools, it is important to document various approaches being adopted here, identify common patterns if any and highlight gaps that need to be addressed. This book aims to provide a more detailed glimpse about how responsible management education is being implemented in some business schools across India and in a few other parts of South East Asia.

Organization of the Book

The book derives from the 6th PRME Asia Forum that was organized at Goa, India, by the Goa Institute of Management to explore why and

[27] Fougere, M., N. Solitander, and S. Young. 2014. "Exploring and Exposing Values in Management Education: Problematizing Final Vocabularies in Order to Enhance Moral Imagination." *Journal of Business Ethics* 120, pp. 175–187.
[28] Waddock, S., and J. M. Lozano. 2013. "Developing More Holistic Management Education: Lessons Learned from Two Programs. "*Academy of learning & Education* 12, no. 2, pp. 265–284.

how responsible management was being integrated into the curriculum of Asian business schools. There were several presentations and discussions at the pre-Forum Teaching Workshop and during the forum on the theme. This book is confined to the learnings from the pre-Forum Workshop on Teaching Responsible Management.

In the pre-Forum workshop, faculty members who taught in Asian (mostly Indian) business schools shared their specific, course-level interventions to promote responsible management. They described the philosophy underlying their courses, the pedagogies adopted to suit the context, some challenges they faced, and their responses. Faculty members, educational administrators, and a few senior executives from well-known organizations participated in the discussions.

The Introduction defines responsible management and leadership and explores why responsible management is needed, how business schools have responded to this need and what challenges they face. Chapter 1 draws from the presentations made at the pre-Forum Workshop to present the drivers of responsible management in Asia and some of the positive responses of Asian business and business schools.

Chapters 2 to 8 of this book present the learnings from the pre-Forum Workshop and from six case studies.

Chapters 2 to 4 share the institute-level interventions to promote responsible management and leadership. Chapter 2 details the journey of Indira Group of Business Studies—the business school attached to a private institution called the Indira Group of Institutes—to integrate responsible management into the curriculum. The process unfolded across three stages: creating awareness about the need for sustainable development, getting people involved in incorporating the concept of sustainability in the curricular and extracurricular activities, reviewing the efforts, and making further revisions. Chapter 3 describes the interventions of the Colegio de San Juan de Letran Calamba—a private, nonprofit university in the Philippines—to inculcate responsible management among its graduates and PhDs. The chapter details how three courses— "Social Responsibility and Good Governance," "Environmental Technology Management," and "Transformational Leadership"—

are delivered across various programs in the graduate school. It describes the pedagogies used in each course, the manner by which the learning activities are facilitated, the learning outcomes, and challenges faced. Chapter 4 briefly describes the vision, mission, and strategies adopted by the Centre for Corporate Sustainability and Innovations (CCSI) at Hang Seng Management College, Hong Kong, to promote sustainability among its stakeholders. Since its birth in 2015, the Centre has been taking steps to promote awareness about the sustainable development goals and enthuse its stakeholders to integrate responsible management and sustainability into their activities.

Chapters 5 to 8 present course-level interventions to promote responsible management. Chapter 5 presents an overview of the course level interventions discussed during the Pre-Forum Workshop. Faculty members from well-known Asian business schools shared their experiences of inculcating responsible management. It details the pedagogies adopted in various courses and the rationale for these pedagogies. Chapter 6 describes the design of the course "Marketing Ethics" offered at the Indian Institute of Management (IIM) Indore—an autonomous business schools setup by the Government of India. The chapter details the course outline besides sharing the instructors' experiences of conducting the course. Chapter 7 describes the experiences of teaching "Ethics in Business" at a well-known university in western India. Given the limited flexibility in changing the university syllabus for the course, the instructor introduces three distinct activities to invigorate and contemporize the course within the confines of the existing syllabus. She discusses the design and conduct of the activities, some challenges faced, and the students' reactions to these activities. Chapter 8 describes the design and conduct of an elective on Rural Marketing offered in the two-year full-time post graduate program in management at a private university called KIIT University in Orissa, India. The chapter especially focuses on the Marketing Opportunity Identification Process (MOIP) module of the course that was introduced to enable participants to become more responsible marketers. It describes the design and conduct of a field project in the MOIP module, the challenges faced in implementing the project, and some outcomes.

Chapter 9 puts together some key learnings from the earlier chapters about why and how responsible management is being inculcated in some Asian business schools. The chapter details the drivers of responsible management and responsible management education. It summarizes key learnings about how these schools are inculcating responsible management and what challenges they face in doing so. Given the novelty and complexity of the concept of responsible management, administrators and educators are still making sense of how to inculcate responsible management. Collaboration with business and other business schools seems key to developing innovative and more effective approaches.

The Six Principles of PRME

Source: www.unprme.org/about-prme/the-six-principles.php

As institutions of higher education involved in the development of current and future managers, we declare our willingness to progress in the implementation, within our institution, of the following Principles, starting with those that are more relevant to our capacities and mission. We will report on progress to all our stakeholders and exchange effective practices related to these principles with other academic institutions:

Principle 1 | Purpose: We will develop the capabilities of students to be future generators of sustainable value for business and society at large and to work for an inclusive and sustainable global economy.

Principle 2 | Values: We will incorporate into our academic activities and curricula the values of global social responsibility as portrayed in international initiatives such as the United Nations Global Compact.

Principle 3 | Method: We will create educational frameworks, materials, processes, and environments that enable effective learning experiences for responsible leadership.

Principle 4 | Research: We will engage in conceptual and empirical research that advances our understanding about the role, dynamics and impact of corporations in the creation of sustainable social, environmental, and economic value.

Principle 5 | Partnership: We will interact with managers of business corporations to extend our knowledge of their challenges in meeting social and environmental responsibilities and to explore jointly effective approaches to meeting these challenges.

Principle 6 | Dialogue: We will facilitate and support dialog and debate among educators, students, business, government, consumers, media, civil society organizations, and other interested groups and stakeholders on critical issues related to global social responsibility and sustainability.

We understand that our own organizational practices should serve as example of the values and attitudes we convey to our students.

CHAPTER 1

Responsible Management: Drivers and Responses Discussed at the Pre-Forum Workshop in the 6th PRME Asia Forum

Ranjini Swamy

Goa Institute of Management

Introduction

In the last decade,[1] there have been shifts in the top ten global risks that are reported annually by the World Economic Forum (WEF). Earlier, the risks were geopolitical (e.g., terrorism) and economic. In recent times, many of these are environmental, societal, or geopolitical risks. In 2015 for instance, the top ten global risks reported as most likely to occur include extreme weather events, natural catastrophes, failure of climate change adaptation, and water crisis.

The changing nature of global risks is a reflection of the *new normal* that business is experiencing and recognizing. These changes could potentially impact the continued economic growth of society and of corporate sector. According to Mr P.S. Narayan, Vice President and Head of

---

[1] This chapter is based on the proceedings of the workshop on Teaching Responsible Management held as part of the 6th PRME Asia Forum at Goa, India in November 2015. The first section of the chapter on "The emerging context of business" was based on the presentation by Mr Narayan of Wipro Ltd.

Sustainability at Wipro Ltd., the top question for business is, "Can we remain isolated from these risks to society and the environment, or do we need to engage with these in a constructive manner? Do we have to choose between economic growth and sustainable progress?" There are several more fundamental and related questions:

- First, what is it that business owes society and planet, if anything at all? (Some suggest that it is enough to create jobs and pay taxes.) Why should an organization think and worry about being responsible? Does this responsibility toward society have strategic fit at all?
- Second, is it possible to be a strong company in a weak society? A company could be a great company but if the society in which it exists is weak, what does that mean for the company? What professional or moral dilemmas does such a situation pose to that company?
- Third, what should be the boundaries of a company's business responsibilities? Where do business responsibilities end and social responsibilities start? Or is that a wrong question? Should it be a spectrum? Two concepts—circular economy and product stewardship—suggest that everyone involved in the life span of the product has to take up responsibility to reduce its adverse environmental, health, and safety impacts.
- Fourth, how can business decisions be informed by long-term forces that are seemingly invisible and peripheral today? A greater understanding of the relationship among the economic, social, and environmental well-being is critical. Are these mutually exclusive or mutually reinforcing?
- Fifth, how should business act toward the social and environmental risks? Are there opportunities embedded that companies or businesses can enrich? How does one integrate social and environmental challenges into business strategy? How can leaders reconcile and find an optimum balance between goals that are seemingly conflicting?
- Sixth, should businesses be led by logics of the markets at all times? How does a company navigate uncertain terrains?

The current measure of economic growth—the Gross Domestic Product (GDP)—does not consider the costs of "externalities" such as pollution and ecosystem loss while calculating growth. As a result, the GDP measure of economic growth could be inflated. New measures of growth, such as the Genuine Progress Indicator (GPI), have emerged in response. The GPI is a weighted index that measures a combination of the costs of pollution, unemployment, ecosystem loss, and so on, and adjusts economic growth against such costs. While the GPI is still work-in-progress, its measure of economic growth diverges from that of the GDP. While economic growth as measured by GDP shows an increasing trend, the growth as measured by GPI does not show such a trend. It appears that the costs borne by society and the environment are increasing.

Drivers of Responsible Management

Intergovernmental agencies like the United Nations have brought together several stakeholders (national governments, civil society, and business) to develop a vision of a safe, just, inclusive and sustainable planet. They identified critical global challenges to attaining this vision—such as extreme poverty, environmental degradation, and unsustainable production/consumption—and have developed sustainable development goals to address each of these. Achieving these goals requires the cooperation of business, government, civil society, and educational institutions. The United Nations has initiated partnerships and dialogues with these stakeholders for the purpose.

Some of the more advanced economies have acknowledged the responsibility of business to society and translated this into new regulatory norms. According to Professor June Qian, School of Economics and Management, Tsinghua University, China, Asian companies desiring to export their products to these advanced economies need to adapt to the new regulatory norms. Adopting the tried-and-tested norms of the home country in the new markets may obstruct performance. Understanding the principles for responsible management prepares Asian businesses for conducting business in the more advanced economies.[2]

---

[2] Based on the presentation and discussion with Prof. June Qian from Tsinghua University in the pre-Forum workshop on Teaching Responsible Management at the 6th PRME Asia forum at Goa in 2015.

Responsible management can also help a business to manage its risks and avail of opportunities while contributing to the sustainable development of society. To achieve this, business needs to review its net impact on society and environment, and take corrective action where needed. Unfortunately, there are several challenges in assessing the net impact of business on society and environment. Professor Raghuram Tata of XLRI Jamshedpur, India, shared some of these challenges during the course of his presentation:[3]

- First, many industry-generated costs, such as destruction of forest cover, are discussed in technical, nonmonetary terms, while many industry-generated benefits are discussed in monetary terms. The lack of comparable language and metrics makes it difficult to accurately assess the net impact of business on society.
- Second, assessments of business impact based on the current anthropocentric definition of sustainability could be partial or incomplete. Such a definition implicitly regards humankind as the central or most important element of existence, especially as opposed to other species.[4] Given this definitional bias, the impact of business on ecosystems beneficial to humankind (such as crops and livestock) could be assessed while its impact on ecosystem services not directly instrumental to humankind may not be assessed. The latter may be incidental to humankind but critical for the survival of other species.

  If a business enterprise requires diversion of forest land for its activities, the net present value of the forest land is computed on the basis of the monetary value of seven ecosystem services in the forest including timber and fuel wood, nontimber forest

---

[3] From the lecture by Prof Raghuram Tata of XLRI Jamshedpur in the Workshop in Teaching Responsible Management at the 6th PRME Asia Forum.
[4] Defined as those aspects of ecosystems utilized (actively or passively) to produce human well-being. The key points are that services must be ecological phenomena and that they do not have to be directly utilized.

products, fodder, bioprospecting,[5] flagship species,[6] and carbon sequestration.[7] Based on the value of these ecosystem services, forest land in India is valued at about Rupees 770,000 per hectare. This valuation excludes other ecosystem services that are not directly useful to humankind.

- Third, the assumptions underlying the valuation of such ecosystem services are contested. In 1997, for instance, a robust global monetized account of the value of the world's ecosystem services and natural capital was proposed. The value of the world's ecosystem services was estimated to be in the range of $16 trillion to $54 trillion per year,[8] the average being around $33 trillion per year. The assumptions underlying such a valuation were not accepted by other economists. The impact of business on the ecosystem services thus remains contentious.

Corporate Responses

Despite the difficulties of measuring impact, there is an increasing acknowledgment that business is impacting and can significantly impact the natural and social systems. If some of the adverse impacts of business are not addressed, survival could be at risk. Some companies have therefore developed policies to address these risks proactively. The following three examples are illustrative:

---

[5] Bioprospecting refers to future opportunities of discovering biochemicals that will be part of the pharma industry.

[6] If there is a tiger or if there is an elephant or a rhinoceros, the value of the forest is manifold more than its ecological services.

[7] A natural or artificial process by which carbon dioxide is removed from the atmosphere and held in a solid or liquid form.

[8] Source: http://community-wealth.org/sites/clone.community-wealth.org/files/downloads/article-costanza-et-al.pdf

Note: The section on "Corporate Responses" is based on the presentation by Prof. Raghu Ram Tata of XLRI Jamshedpur and discussions during the session he led during the workshop on Teaching Responsible Management at the 6th PRME Asia Forum at Goa in 2015.

Coca-Cola has developed a global integrated water strategy to become water neutral by 2020. To achieve this, they engage with other stakeholders who are involved in water management or water use.

Wipro Ltd. has programmes to improve the biodiversity on its campuses.

ITC Ltd., a diversified Indian company, has invested in a social forestry initiative to ensure sustained supply of raw materials for its paper division. It collaborates with communities to raise plantations of soft wood that the company uses as raw material. There are several business benefits: (a) an assured supply of raw material; (b) a reputation as carbon-positive and water-positive company.[9] For the past five years, they are also a waste-neutral company.

Many companies are now capturing the value created through such initiatives either in their sustainability reports or (less frequently) in their profit and loss accounts. Besides recognition in the markets, the sustainability reports also serve as signaling devices to the stakeholders. A few companies like PUMA have gone beyond such reports. In 2011, PUMA became the first company in the world to develop and report the "environmental profit and loss account." It reports the environmental externalities caused in its entire supply chain, puts a monetary value to these externalities, and identifies where these externalities are concentrated. The company committed itself to reduce its global ecological footprints by 25 percent by the year 2015 and achieved most of the goals. They have helped other companies like Wipro Ltd. to do such an exercise.

The question is why would companies like PUMA reveal everything about their adverse impact on the environment? They could restrict themselves to producing a sustainability report. It raises very interesting questions in the classroom: Is there a strategic reason behind these initiatives? Who drives the initiative—external stakeholders or internal stakeholders like the chief executive officer (CEO)? If it is a single leader's initiative, say the CEO's, will this get institutionalized? How can the outcomes of such

---

[9] As the plantations absorb carbon, ITC claims that they are carbon-positive company. And as the forest recharges ground water, ITC claims it is a water-positive company.

initiatives be measured? Can all the outcomes be converted into accurate monetary measures? More generally, can industry realize "zero footprint" on the ecology? This may require that the materials and resources move seamlessly across the economy. That would be a big challenge for the global companies.[10]

Businesses are taking more interest in the emerging ecosystem services markets. One such market—Bioprospecting—has some pharmaceutical companies paying the tribals in Amazon forests to not destroy forests, because the industry realizes that future biochemicals might come from that forest. Bioprospecting has made a beginning in India also.

Implications for Education

Educational institutions can promote responsible management and thereby contribute to the development of an inclusive, safe, just and sustainable society. Asian business schools, for instance, can help generate and disseminate knowledge regarding why responsible management is important in the Asian context, what it means to be responsible and how business can contribute to the betterment of society. They can help inculcate the appropriate competencies among future managers through revised curricula. What competencies must be inculcated among future managers to ensure that they take responsibility for the wellbeing of business, society and the natural environment?[11] The following competencies were presented during the workshop:

- The ability to understand the complex inter-linkages among the natural systems like energy, water etc., that exist independent of human involvement and between the natural, human and economic systems.

---

[10] From the lecture by Prof Raghuram Tata of XLRI Jamshedpur in the Workshop in Teaching Responsible Management at the 6th PRME Asia Forum.

[11] This section is based on the presentation of Mr. Narayan, Wipro Ltd., during the workshop on Teaching Responsible Management, at the 6th PRME Asia Forum at Goa, India, in 2015.

- An awareness of the externalities created by business and their impact on business, society and the natural environment.
- The ability to think about and act upon complex problems in a holistic manner. This could require drawing on multiple stakeholder perspectives to diagnose complex problems and develop action plans to resolve them.
- Compassion and an empathy for people who experience inequity or unfairness in society.

Institute-Level Responses of Business Schools

Inculcating competencies for responsible management and leadership requires the development of new curricular and co-curricular interventions, as well as appropriate pedagogies. Several business schools in Asia appear to have initiated institute-level interventions to promote responsible management.

Professor Radha Sharma presented some of the curricular and extra-curricular initiatives at MDI Gurgaon, India.[12] The mission of the institute is to create cutting-edge management capability at individual and organizational levels through value-based education, action-centric research, and value-added consulting. The institute responded to the calls for sustainable development by jointly[13] organizing an international conference on the social responsibility of business. Conference participants deliberated on how to introduce social and business responsibility in business school curriculum in India. It was, however, difficult to convince people of the importance of sustainable development in those days.

In 2002, with support from British Council India, MDI set up the Centre for Corporate Governance to do research and promote curriculum development in that area. Faculty members of MDI acquired various

---

[12] Based on the presentation by Prof. Radha Sharma, MDI, Gurgaon, in the Workshop on Teaching Responsible Management at the 6th PRME Asia Forum, 2015.

[13] Along with TERI, UN volunteers, UNDP, and the New Academy of Business, UK.

Note: the section on "Institute level responses of Business Schools" is based on the presentation by Prof. Radha Sharma, MDI, Gurgaon, in the Workshop on Teaching Responsible Management at the 6th PRME Asia Forum, 2015.

certifications in the area of social responsibility. At the time there was need to develop case studies on corporate governance in Indian companies. With the support from United Nations Development Programme (UNDP), the Centre developed and publicized several case studies in the form of a book. Later, it partnered with publishing houses to publish more case studies. The Centre also developed executive programs on corporate governance for board members.

It encouraged scholarship in the area of Corporate Governance through the PhD program. Many PhD scholars researched in the area of Corporate Social Responsibility (CSR), corporate governance, and well-being. Faculty members also contributed to knowledge generation through research in the areas of well-being, gender issues, green management, sustainability, and so on. They participated in advocacy, both at national and international fora, and received recognition for it.

On the curriculum front, the six principles of the Principles for Responsible Management Education (PRME)were integrated into the PhD program. Responsible Management was integrated into the MBA program through (a) modules on responsible management in existing courses such as organizational behavior, leadership and emotional Intelligence; (b) full-credit courses on energy management, sustainable energy development, business ethics, corporate governance and corporate social responsibility. The institute has also introduced a two-year postgraduate program on energy management, where it offers courses on management of energy and environment and sustainable energy development. Students learnt about social responsibility through various interactive pedagogies such as case studies, project work, advocacy, and research. They regularly interacted with representatives of nongovernmental organizations (NGOs) and industry, organized blood donation camps, ran health camps for thalassemia patients, and organized fund-raising for social projects such as building toilets for girl children in schools.

Summary and Implications

In sum, this chapter provided a brief overview of some key drivers of responsible management in Asia. Research by the World Economic Forum has showed that social and environmental risks could significantly impact the survival and growth of business. There is a need to understand these risks and measure their potential impact on business. Measures of these impacts are still work in progress. Research is also helping measure the impact of business on society and the environment. With greater clarity about the impact of business on society, governments of advanced economies have developed stricter regulatory norms. Export-oriented Asian companies realize they have to adapt to these new norms. This could be driving some of them to understand responsible management.

If business has to take responsibility for its existing or potential impact on society and the environment, it needs responsible managers and leaders. Business schools need to revise their curricular and co-curricular interventions in the light of this need. The chapter presented some details of how the MDI, Gurgaon, has integrated responsible management across its academic and cocurricular activities. Responsible management has been introduced as stand-alone courses in a discipline (e.g., business ethics) or as a module/session within existing discipline-based courses (e.g., organizational behavior). Through the Centre for Corporate Governance, MDI has introduced cocurricular activities for students to promote responsible management. It has integrated responsible management into research, case study writing, teaching, training, and advocacy. It also has introduced a new postgraduate program on energy management.

PART I

Case Studies on Institute-Level Interventions to Promote Responsible Management

CHAPTER 2

Indira School of Business Studies in Pursuit of Responsible Management Education

Renu Bhargava and B. S. Guha

Indira School of Business Studies, India

Background

Indira School of Business Studies (ISBS) is part of the Indira Group of Institutes (IGI), a private educational institution in Pune, India, which offers education from primary school to postgraduate level. The IGI was set up more than 20 years ago by the Shri Chanakya Education Society (SCES) to offer "affordable, accessible, and available" education to the aspiring youth who have been denied such opportunities. This was seen as a contribution to society, given that educational institutes at the time were inadequate to meet the requirements of a growing, young population. The focus of IGI was on providing higher education, that is, graduate and postgraduate education. Its programs were approved by the University of Pune, India (now called the Savitribai Phule Pune University).

The *ISBS* was set up as an autonomous center in IGI, to provide management education. The Trustees of ISBS (see Annexure 2.1) strongly mandated holistic value addition. Under the able stewardship of the founding chairperson and advisory board, ISBS recognized and acted on the governing principle—"Make a good person first, a good manager will follow." It was recognized by the All India Council for Technical Education (AICTE) in 2006.

The ISBS has consciously worked toward weaving the theme of socially relevant and responsible education into the curriculum. The curriculum was enriched with activities that aimed at personality development and increased awareness of social concerns in equal measure. Students were rated on their personality development and academic performance. Placement forms an important milestone for both the students and the institution. ISBS has always taken great pride in offering responsible citizens and mature, eager candidates to its "clients". This has served the primary stakeholders well. This case study outlines the path taken by ISBS to incorporate the Principles for Responsible Management Education into the curriculum. Annexure 2.2 provides an overview of the path ISBS took to integrate responsible management and sustainability into its academic activities.

Interventions and Outcomes

Phase 1 (2006 to 2009)

The Trustees of ISBS recognized several important trends in society that led them to believe that the institute needed to build responsible citizens. The increasing media reports on ethical scams appeared to be the result of a business model that emphasized unfettered economic growth at the cost of human rights and the ecology. There was an emerging global concern about the threats to human rights and ecology. Numerous bodies, both (inter)governmental and nongovernmental, were opening up to a discourse and dialogue on these issues. United Nations (UN) institutions such as the United Nations Framework Convention on Climate Change (UNFCCC) and United Nations Educational, Social, and Cultural Organization (UNESCO) provided detailed information on the present status of human rights and climate change. They helped create broad consensus on the Millennium Development Goals to be achieved to make the world a sustainable society. This led to new/modified corporate governance guidelines to bring some sensible control on how companies should be run. Stakeholder rather than shareholder concerns began to be voiced.

While the role of educational institutions appeared clear, ISBS was not clear how this could be achieved. The challenge was how to impart the "wisdom" of responsible and sustainable business through education. The stakeholders of ISBS voiced several concerns in this regard: the lack of deliverable and "formalized" knowledge on responsible management and sustainable development, the short time in which such knowledge had to be imparted (four semesters over two years), the lack of faculty training on the theme, and the difficulty in making major changes in the syllabus that was determined by the University. Yet, there was acknowledgment that responsible management and sustainable development were every manager's responsibility. It was in this context that ISBS began its journey to incorporate Responsible Management Education.

A central advisory body called the Advisory Council was created and duly empowered to advance the integration of responsible management and sustainable development. The implementation would occur in phases. ISBS recognized that the outcome should reflect in an increased sense of social responsibility within the individual and an awareness of global ethical values. To help achieve this, faculty members and administrators needed to become aware about the theme of responsible management and sustainable development.

Creating Awareness among Faculty Members. Common mandatory programs were conducted to sensitize all faculty members about responsible management. These included a 45-hour module on responsible management, full-day seminars and shorter duration seminars on failures of governance (frauds), emerging practices in corporate social responsibility (CSR), information on the *The Brundtland Report, The United Nation's Millennium Development Goals,* and *The Global Compact.* Recognized speakers addressed faculty members through the newly established "Gyan-Ganga" Seminars. (Please see Annexure 2.3 for some of the topics discussed in these seminars.) In "Book Report" sessions, faculty members led seminars on contemporary publications in the area of responsible management or sustainable development (for example, a discussion of *Peter Senge's The Necessary Revolution,* and *John Elkington's Cannibals with Forks).* IGO also organized Industry-Academia workshops in Mumbai on "The Learning Organization," one of

which was facilitated by *Prof. Senge.* Prof. Senge explained the neb-
ulous concept of sustainability. Senior alumni and respected managers were also invited to mentor the introduction of Sustainable
Development into the curriculum.

Creating Awareness among Students. To create awareness among students, ISBS held "workshops" on responsible management and
sustainability during the Induction Program. Films such as Al Gore's
"An Inconvenient Truth," video clips from *C. K. Prahalad's* "Fortune
at the bottom of the pyramid," and exercises were organized for the
purpose. The sessions were rounded off with competitive quizzes to
generate higher engagement. A "certificate course" on sustainability
was delivered to students during the semesters.

Students were encouraged to work as volunteers with *Habitat for
Humanity*—an NGO that builds homes and communities across
the world—to build a village for the underprivileged people in
Malavali, a place 25 kilometers from Pune. About 1,000 people
from different countries participated in *"shram-daan[1]"* to build the
village. Materials were contributed by local industry and the project
was coordinated by Habitat for Humanity. About 100 ISBS students
were invited to join as "unskilled" helpers in the project. Celebrities
like Steve Waugh, Brad Pitt, and others worked alongside on the
project. This experience gave the initiative many "ambassadors."
ISBS leveraged IGI's industry contacts for sustainability-related
seminars, guest lectures, and the like.

From these first steps, ISBS chalked out the following plans to improve
student awareness about sustainability: (a) organize at least one
"mega" event on sustainability through the students' forum to
link sustainability with fun; (b) encourage students' participation
in city-based activities such as tree-planting drives and "Save Fuel"
demonstrations; (c) increase participation of students in the university's CSR activities; (d) continue the Certificate Course on Sustainability; (e) encourage students to collaborate with Confederation
of Indian Industry-Young India Initiative (CII-Yi) and the local
industry, to add sustainable value to society through their Social

---

[1] Voluntary contribution of labor for a public cause

Responsibility Council. (Please see Annexure 2.3 for a list of some activities initiated by this Council.) Students have started a campus project on recycling waste, as part of the "Save our Earth" initiative at ISBS. They use technology to convert the campus waste into compost for utilization as manure.

Developing Curricular Interventions: Interactive brainstorming sessions are conducted with the faculty members of ISBS on how the concept of sustainable development and responsible management could be incorporated into the B school curriculum and into the institute's research agenda. Faculty were required to teach Responsible Management in their respective "domains of expertise."

In the first semester, ISBS introduced a desk-researched project, called "Term Project for Cross-Functional Integration" (TPCFI). Students were introduced to the basic concept of Business Performance and Triple Bottom Line (TBL). A model "presentation" was made by the course facilitator demonstrating the link between sustainability and business performance. Thereafter, student-teams were given two weeks to prepare a similar presentation on assigned companies. Each presentation was discussed in class, following which the teams were asked to submit an e-report. Students were evaluated based on Presentation, Report, Viva (for the team members), and a multiple-choice-question-type test for all students.

A Certificate Course on Sustainability was introduced in the curriculum of the postgraduate diploma course(s). Knowledge of theoretical constructs (for example, triple bottom line) was complemented by practical knowledge through interaction with internationally acclaimed experts in workshops. For instance, in 2006, the head, Unilever (South East Asia), was invited to highlight Unilever's efforts toward sustainability and to explain its philosophy: "Good Business can only come from Good society." ISBS hosted a series of seminars on "sustainability" by leading management thinkers from industry and nongovernment organizations (NGOs) to spread awareness about the concept of sustainability.

As sustainable solutions required innovative approaches, ISBS introduced Seminars on Innovation Management that were led by business stalwarts from international business. In 2008, a course

"Harnessing Creativity and Innovation" was offered to students, to promote individual creative thinking as well as manage creativity in a group setting. A second certified course on innovation management was offered annually by internationally acclaimed experts. Such initiatives helped students discover business opportunities in multicultural settings.

IGI also held a workshop for its various stakeholders from industry and academia on "Solving Tough Problems" as its effort toward community outreach. This was attended by representatives of industry, politics, social organizations, and academics. The Chairman of Confederation of Indian Industries (CII), Pune Chapter, shared how the CII evolved (jointly with the Maharashtra State Electricity Board) the now famous "Pune Model" to enhance the peak-power capability of Pune city.

Students' participation in Sustainability Electives in Program and in the corporate social responsibility and community service initiatives of the institute is considered for assessing their preparedness for campus recruitment processes. "Placement Preparedness" ratings were influenced positively by participation and performance in this domain. The rating impacts the shortlisting of students for placement in particular companies.

Promoting Research on Responsible Management and Sustainable Development. The Research and Development Centre (IRDC) encouraged faculty to do research on social and sustainable causes. As a result, 10 papers were presented by ISBS faculty in recognized forums. The IRDC also assisted the Maharashtra Industrial Development Corporation (MIDC) in conducting a socioeconomic survey of three villages from Satara District, Maharashtra, to determine the demographic profile and socioeconomic status of farmers who were likely to be displaced by the MIDC projects, recommend a customized rehabilitation package and research the best practices in compensating farmers for land acquisition. The IRDC's recommendations formed the foundation for MIDC's proposed rehabilitation policy. The IRDC also worked with *Yashada,* Child Labor Centre to document case studies on the elimination of child labor. With ILO funding, IRDC has documented 24 best practices on the issue in four districts of Maharashtra.

Review: The emphasis of these interventions was on creating awareness and ensuring repeated involvement of the academic community in sustainability initiatives, rather than on the precise measurement of effectiveness. Administrators, faculty, and the students were sensitized to the theme of sustainability through several activities. On review, ISBS realized that the effort was not as "balanced" as had been targeted. In fact, there was a groundswell of concern among the faculty and administrators that many of these initiatives were causing more "distraction" than adding to the students' development. Priority to academics was being jeopardized. The interventions were perceived as dispersed rather than focussed, and very unevenly applied across functions and programs. In 2009, the directors of the different colleges assessed the contribution of the inputs to the development of students as "responsible managers." The approach appeared to have inadvertently sent out a signal that "sustainability" was an added topping, an optional extra, to the "main" academic and personality development. The rough and ready assessment of outcome at the end of 2009 may be summarized as follows:

"Return on Effort": PRME Principles (2009)

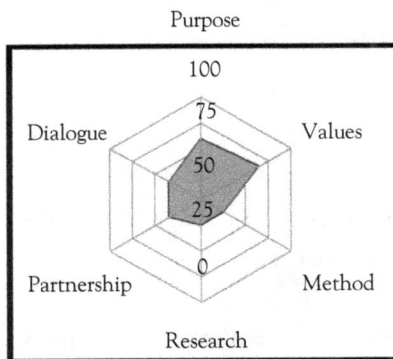

External developments however continued to reinforce the importance of developing responsible managers. The sub-prime crisis in the United States and the rise of fraudulent, "unacceptable" corporate practices emphasized the need for governance and ethics. Internationally, the limited progress on the Millennium Goals datelined for 2015 indicated the need for concerted efforts to build responsible managers.

ISBS felt the need to reorient its mission to deliver "Responsible Management Education." Given the limited duration of the program, any meaningful impact on student engagement had to be intense, multidimensional, and persistent. There was need for some "freedom of choice" (for students and faculty alike!); at the same time, it was necessary to communicate a "no escape" clause. On the curriculum front, there was need to integrate sustainability more fully into the course work. To achieve this, there was need for more concerted efforts to enhance knowledge in the domains of CSR, ethics, and sustainability. More credits needed to be allotted for courses on sustainability, corporate governance, and ethics. Also needed was a capstone course on sustainability in the third/fourth semester. Making changes in the syllabus could, however, be challenging. Until faculty were available with the required expertise, ISBS would have to access expertise from outside for the conduct of courses and seminars on sustainability.

On the research front, there was need for more research and dialogue on sustainability. More seminars were needed on industry practices in the area of sustainability. ISBS would also encourage summer internships for students in the area of CSR and governance. While extracurricular activities would continue and complement the academic programs, it was important not to sacrifice academic rigor and industry readiness of students. There was an acknowledgment of the need to assess the outcome of these initiatives.

Phase 2 (2009 to 2013)

This section will share what ISBS did to operationalize "responsible management education" in the next five years.

> *Curricular changes*: The certificate course on sustainability called "Term Project for Cross-functional Integration" (TPCFI) was discontinued in the program. There was limited data available in the public domain on the triple bottom line (TBL) performance of companies. Also, given the limited exposure to sustainability,

students tended to focus on the traditional indicators of financial performance. Reports on financial performance were already being done in Semester II in another course. ISBS therefore discontinued the desk-researched project. Instead, it introduced pre-term foundation lectures titled "Introduction to Business and Management," "Concept of a modern Corporation," and "Critical Perspectives."

There were suggestions for integrating sustainability in every functional domain in the curriculum, be it marketing, finance, or HRM. The following additions were finally made:

- A course on CSR and ethics was introduced in Semester I as a full-credit course (3 credits). The course required students to do desk research and analyze case studies.
- Toward the end of Semester II, a seminar on "Management—21st Century" was introduced[2] (additionally, the Digitalization of Business and consequent models were covered). A weekly cocurricular session was introduced in Semester II.[3]
- A full credit course called "Sector Study Seminar" was introduced to expose students to newer concepts related to sustainability such as triple-bottom line. The marks obtained on the course were included in the Academic Report Card, even though there was no formal end-term examination.
- Elective courses on sustainability, CSR, and "Green" approaches were introduced in Semester III under General Management, HRM, Marketing, and Finance specializations.

---

[2] Discusses the paradigm shift in thinking—kicked off by Drucker's "Management in the 21st Century" followed by Senge's "The Necessary Revolution," Porter's "Corporate Shared Value" and approach toward *The Circular Economy.*

[3] Certain skill-based training included in every semester prepared students for corporate world and such training was encompassed within what is called cocurricular sessions. Career and Leadership Development Program (CLDP) formed part of the cocurricular sessions. Students were assessed in these skills after the completion of training imparted with "Placement worthiness" being the outcome expected.

- "Innovation Management" was introduced as a certificate course in Semester III to help students learn how to think "out-of-box" and drive sustainability.
- A "Capstone" dissertation-oriented course was introduced in Semester IV to promote in-depth understanding of sustainability.

Extracurricular Activities: ISBS intensified its association and partnership with several local and national associations in its bid to enhance the dialogue on sustainability.[4] ISBS students regularly participated in community service initiatives with NGOs. The engagement with PRME and the Global Compact intensified. In a conscious administrative decision, self-generated, "one-off" initiatives were not encouraged. The Entrepreneurship-Cell on Campus (Arohan), and the Social Responsibility Council on Campus promote a greater understanding of and participation in sustainability initiatives. A seminar on the theme of *Sustainable Strategies in Dynamic Business Environment* is organized annually to bring together academics, students and corporate professionals to discuss trends, directions and new challenges on the theme of responsible management and sustainability.

Review: As with any interlinked activity, the design and evaluation of the sustainability initiatives became more complex and time consuming. There was need to assess the impact and outcomes of various initiatives such as community outreach. However, an undue emphasis on hard evidence at times could overlook qualitative outcomes of responsible management education and may restrict self-driven initiatives of students.

---

[4] Some agencies were local—such as the Mahratta Chamber of Commerce Industries and Agriculture, Pune (MCCIA) and the Pune Management Association. Others—such as the Federation of Indian Chamber of Commerce and Industry (FICCI, New Delhi), the Confederation of Indian Industries, Pune (CII), the National Human Resource Development Pune, Chapter (NHRD), and the National Entrepreneurship Network (NEN)—were national bodies.

Some of the challenges faced in the first phase of implementation-limited stakeholder awareness and involvement, varying degree of integration of sustainability in the curriculum and variations in the quality of interventions- continued into the second phase. Yet the Institute had moved toward a greater but gradual inclusion of responsible management and sustainable development in its curriculum. A few faculty members had completed their doctoral studies in sustainability and allied domains. Faculty papers and publication on the theme of sustainability had risen. Consequently, ISBS faculty were better able to offer electives on sustainability. They were able to steer co-curricular activities on the theme. New faculty members with expertise in sustainability were also added. The students' requirement for greater focus was also addressed. Faculty participation in steering cocurricular activities also increased. The ISBS decided to induct new faculty with specialization and experience in sustainability.

In 2013, the management reviewed the efforts to integrate responsible management and sustainability. The "progress" was charted in the following figure. There was a fair increase in the "input" side, but it was not clear whether the inputs were meeting the PRME objectives in providing "responsible management education." There was need to engage more vigorously with industry to assess the effectiveness of efforts and realign the direction of efforts.

"Return on Effort": PRME Principles (2009 to 2013)

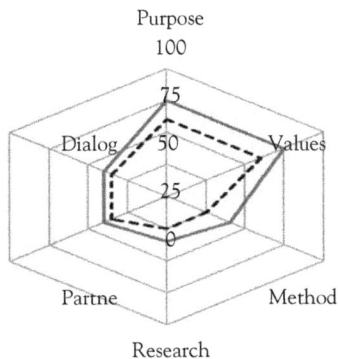

The "journey" to integrate responsible management and sustainability was very rough. There were failures, dead-ends, and on many occasions, feelings of extreme frustration. The principal learnings from the experience were as follows:

- Keep experimenting and keep the "excitement" going. At the same time, allow for "comfort" of choice through diversity of activities.
- Demonstrate/continuously signal to all that the values of responsibility and sustainability are as important as "lecture Room" experiences, grades, and the conventional trappings of "education"—and there is no escape. Firmly shut the gate to prevent "leakages."
- Be prepared for failure and skepticism, and for continuous improvisations. The (limited) syllabus extensions and the various co- and extracurricular activities have to be constantly improvised. There is a great paucity of scholarly work but an abundance of information and ideas on the net (e.g., TED Talks). Pedagogy must adjust to this fact.
- Outcomes will manifest over time as there are no immediate results. As "responsibility" is an attitude, it is advisable to attempt to evaluate "successes" in terms of student attitudes. It is very difficult to develop a rigorous scale to measure attitudes of responsibility. Perhaps, with time and with the adoption of "outcome"-based assessments, a more rigorous assessment of such outcomes will emerge.

Phase 3 (2014 Onwards)

In the third phase, there were several changes made. First, there was a shift toward establishing partnerships with industry. Second, there was a gradual (and ongoing) shift from "input-based" to "outcome-based" teaching and learning. Program and course objectives are being redefined, pedagogy reworked, and evaluation modalities are being changed to make for more insightful and responsible managers. There is a greater desire to measure and assess the **outcome** of the efforts (and inputs) to understand the efficiency and effectiveness of approaches.

ISBS hopes to steer the outcome-based education (OBE) in the next five years. While this period may not be smooth sailing, it would ultimately enable accreditation of the programs in the future. The OBE model focuses on learning outcomes (i.e., what the learner can demonstrate at the end of a learning activity) and on competence. The relationship between learning outcomes and competences is a complex area and is a subject of some debate and considerable confusion. Nevertheless, the ISBS feels that these can be overcome by developing appropriate technology platforms.

Giselle Weybrecht's report at the recent PRME Global Forum at New York served as an important reminder of what outcomes business schools needed to deliver. According to her, *"Business schools should become knowledgeable in what business needs are in the area of sustainability today, and prepare for what they may be in the future"*. There was need for *"... a growing stream of well-grounded and ethically responsible professional practitioners and leaders in every field of public life and endeavour...."*

Annexure 2.1

The Trustees of ISBS

Dr. Tarita Shanker (Chairperson, SCES)

".....The philosophy, governance and value systems of business are witnessing a sea change and plenty of its repercussions are being felt across the globe. India cannot isolate itself from such dynamic, global environment. This is the time to adopt the changes we perceive. Such dynamics should result in better professionalism and inherent strength of a competitive economy.... "

Chetan Wakalkar (Managing Trustee, SCES)

Welcome to the second decade of the 21st Century!!! The world's emergence from recession, even though slow and fragmented, is accepted by all. Every economic crisis in history has brought about breakthroughs in industries, science, and technology. The recent crisis has stimulated thoughts and inspired the international community to make new explorations regarding development models. Growth and integration of a global, increasingly free-market economy has raised the standard of competition in all sectors providing goods and services. On the other hand, management professionals from India are in good demand in international market. Private sector today offers rapid advancement to result-oriented professionals. The daunting complexity of the challenges that confront us would be overwhelming if we were to depend only on existing knowledge, traditional resources, and conventional approaches.

Chanakya says "As soon as fear approaches near, attack and destroy it." This philosophy is enshrined in the soul of Indira Group and enlivened by our lifeblood, that is, faculty and students. We have identified this paradigm shift of managing today's business and therefore always strive to instill the ability of speedy decision-making in resources deployed, managing diversity, searching right direction of knowledge management for the people, and finally social responsibility awareness in our students. Quoting the ancient Chinese strategist Sun Tzu, "Rules of war never change—only weapons change," our tomorrow's corporate warriors will fight for market share and market domination by converting previous knowledge and experience into today's competencies required for best possible strategies. Here we are committed to supply a growing stream of well-grounded and ethically responsible professional practitioners and leaders in every field of public life and endeavor.

(General address on the IGI website)

Annexure 2.2

The journey of ISBS toward inculcating responsibility

	Context	Challenges	Action taken	Key outcomes
Phase: 1 (2006 to 2009)	(a) Emergence of sustainability trend	(a) Exposure to sustainability and direction for faculty	Threefold action plan to improve exposure, Initially with low degree of integration with curriculum	Substantial improvement on the two principles of purpose and values
	(b) Increased expectation from B schools to incorporate sustainability-related aspects into curriculum	(b) Low stakeholder awareness about sustainability and low response	(a) Awareness about sustainability through workshops, other stand-alone events	
	(c) Limited awareness among the stakeholders about sustainability		(b) Hands-on involvement of faculty and students in activities through participation in volunteering	
	(d) Realization about the significance of sustainability		(c) Certificate course on sustainability. Encouraged faculty and students to engage in research in the related theme.	
Phase: 2 (2010 to 2013)	(a) ISBS becomes a member of PRME	(a) Reviews phase 1. Identifies areas of improvement	(a) Offer choice-based curriculum.	Improved performance on dialogue, methods, and research (principles for responsible management)

	(b) Increased stakeholder emphasis on sustainability and value-based education		(b) Integrate sustainability more fully into the curriculum, in relevant courses	
	© Increased student- and faculty -awareness and buy-in		(c) Push for academic and industry tie-ups for research	Continuous improvement process
Phase: 3 (2014 onwards)	(a) Emphasis on quality systems and accreditation in education	Review of phase 2. Asymmetric buy in by internal stakeholders Measurement challenges	(a) Define programed outcomes	
	(b) Quality measurement in education through outcome-based teaching and learning		(b) Align curriculum to achieve the defined outcomes	
	(c) Internal institutional drive for accreditation.		(c) Integrate digital platform for seamless measurement	

Annexure 2.3

Topics Addressed in "Gyan-Ganga" Lectures

Mr. B. G. Verghese (2010)
Senior journalist, author, and press adviser to Mrs. Indira Gandhi
"ECONOMIC GAINS WITH SOCIAL STRAINS: THE WAY OUT"

Dr. Chandra Hariharan (2010)
CEO, Biodiversity Conservation India Ltd., Magsaysay Award Winner
"SUSTAINABLE DEVELOPMENT: BUILDING BLOCKS FOR SENSIBLE LIVING"

Justice Santosh Hegde (2011)
Ex-judge, Supreme Court of India, and ex-chairman, Lok-Ayukt of Karnataka
PROBITY IN PUBLIC LIFE: NEED OF THE HOUR

Dr. Vandana Shiva (2011)
Environmental Activist, Nobel Peace Prize Nominee 2005
GLOBAL WARMING and GM FOODS: IS ECONOMIC DEVELOPMENT MISREADING RISK?

Mr. Rajendra Singh, (2012)
Waterman of India, Magsaysay Awarded
INDIA'S WATER WOES : SOLUTIONS TEMPLATE

Dr. Subramanian Swamy (2013)
Ex-Harvard Prof., Economist, Senior BJP leader
YOUTH AT THE CROSSROAD: THE ROAD AHEAD

Maj Gen. Ian Cardozo (2014)
Chairman Rehabilitation Council of India, Decorated War Hero
MAKING SERVICE BEFORE SELF WORK

Mr. Mahroof Raza (2014)
Strategy and Security Expert
SECURITY CHALLENGES and ECONOMIC GROWTH

Annexure 2.4

Some Activities Initiated by Students Through the Social Responsibility Council

Tree Plantation Drive (Annual)

With vast deforestation, our Institute takes upon itself to plant trees regularly in parks around Pune City.

River Cleaning Drive (Annual)

The ever-increasing population coupled with the domestic as well as industrial pollution has resulted in the rivers being polluted, thereby destroying aquatic life and causing acute scarcity of potable drinking water. In this regard, an effort was undertaken by Indira Yi net by cleaning river with active participation of 200 staff members and students.

Make A Wish Foundation

In association with Yi Pune Chapter, our institute organized "Make a Wish Come True." It was an effort aimed at bringing smile on the faces of deprived children (orphans) and to help others realize their responsibility toward fellow human beings. The funds collected during the campaign have been handed over to the orphanage in Pune.

Earth My Valentine

The Valentine day is celebrated by the students of Indira Group in a unique way, wherein the "valentine" is the Mother Earth. It is our effort to appreciate the resources provided by nature and to conserve them.

Breath

Smoking is pleasure for a moment and a pain for life. "Breath" is an anti-smoking campaign carried out by our students annually, during which they present slides and approach the common man to make him aware of the consequences of smoking.

Sankalp

It is a commitment for helping those who are rendered helpless. It is an annual campaign to, for example, rehabilitate the migrants from Kashmir, where donations are collected from willing donors and channeled to the needy; assistance is sent to drought-affected regions; aid is sent to earthquake-affected regions; and the like.

Tsunami Relief

Nature's power to the extremes of negativity for human race could be seen in the incident of tsunami tragedy, where both lives and property were victims. Students of Indira School of Business Studies took the initiative to pool finance from friends, relatives, faculty, and even corporate to contribute to the Tsunami relief fund. Students also extended their service in the affected locations, providing medicine and survival aids to those ravaged by the storm.

Exposure: Similarly, the principal ongoing initiatives in this respect are:

"Arohan"

Indira School of Business Studies Entrepreneurial-Cell (E-Cell: Arohan) operates through a student body, which promotes entrepreneurship among students. The effort is to create employment generators rather than employment seekers. In an economy such as India, a sustainable economic environment requires that a vast majority of youth become employed to create a sustained employable job environment.

Students make initiatives wherein they invite eminent entrepreneurs to deliver lectures to educate students about the joys and challenges of entrepreneurship.

ISBS E-Cell has initiated the process of actively incubating start-up ideas by linking the right investors with the right entrepreneurs through its annual National Event, "*IndiaPreneur.*"

Business plan competitions are held annually in collaboration with Venture Capitalist Firm, such as IndiaCo Ltd, National Entrepreneurship Network, and CII-Young Indians (Pune Chapter), and ISBS witnesses renowned Industrialists as panelists to assess the worthiness of the business plans. The winning teams have been from institutes such as Indian Institute of Technology, New Delhi, who take away prizes such as INR 125,000, and receive funding from venture capitalist funds for feasible plans.

CHAPTER 3

The Colegio De San Juan De Letran Calamba, Philippines: Nurturing and Shaping Professionals Toward Social Orientation and Care of Creations

Ruel V. Maningas

Assistant Vice President for Academics and Former Dean of Graduate School, Colegio de San Juan de Letran Calamba, Philippines

Melchor C. Morandarte

Letran Calamba

Reynaldo R. Robles**

Background

Two of the most pressing concerns of the 21st century are the increased number of poor people and the increased threats to the natural environment. The UN Millennium Development Goals (MDGs) has taken its torch to mitigate if not totally resolve these two issues, with various strategies and programs implemented over the past decades. While there has been significant progress reported over the past decade, these issues continue to be challenges. Higher educational institutions have emerged as core stakeholders to achieve the Sustainable Development Goals and thereby realize an inclusive and sustainable society. Focussing on the goals relating to poverty eradication, quality education, lifelong opportunities and sustainable use of natural resources can help reduce poverty and environmental degradation (PRME, 2015).

The Philippines has its share of societal challenges. The political turmoil brought about by two people power revolutions has set a clear tone for various stakeholders in the society to keep a tight watch on how the country is governed, and how ethical leadership is practiced in both the public and private sectors. The first people power revolution in 1986 was a result of the oppression of freedom, massive graft and corruption in the government, and life-threatening abuses by the government since the Martial Law proclamation in 1972.[1] In 2001, there was the second people's protest against the corruption by political leaders and the process by which the leader was impeached. These peaceful revolutions created a sense of pride among the citizens. However, it also raised hard questions about democratic choices, rule of law, and stability and order. Although unrehearsed and nonviolent, such protests were seen as indicative of the ambiguity of Philippine democratic practices and the frailty of Filipino political institutions.[2]

The peaceful revolutions in times of crisis demonstrate the importance given by the society to responsible management. While economic growth is key, the people also want corporate governance and accountability of political and other institutions to the public. The critical discourse is how leaders and managers from the growth sectors are nurtured to be socially responsible and accountable in governing their organizations. How and what then is the role of business schools, the graduate schools in particular, in the process of mainstreaming professionals in responsible management?

---

[1] www.philippine-history.org/edsa-people-power-revolution.htm, retrieved 23 August 2016.

[2] www.asj.upd.edu.ph/mediabox/archive/ASJ-39-1-2-2003/gonzalez.pdf, retrieved August 23, 2016

The Institution

The Colegio de San Juan de Letran Calamba is a Catholic, private, non-stock, and nonprofit higher educational institution established in March 1979. Gaining its autonomy from Letran Manila (established in 1620) in 1986, Letran Calamba stands as the first institution of higher learning established by the Dominican Province of the Philippines. It offers primary, secondary, tertiary, and postgraduate level of education with almost 6,000-student population.

Letran Calamba envisions itself as a university, a center of science and technology, as well as a vital formation center in the religious and socio-economic development of the region by 2025. It is committed to the total human development; better quality of life of its students, faculty, and employees; and the promotion of a genuine community through an education that is Filipino, Dominican, and Christian in orientation. To realize the institutional vision and to fulfill its mission, Letran Calamba commits itself to deliver consistently quality education to its students and quality service to its stakeholders through a relevant outcomes-based instruction, sustained research and community extension culture, and continually improved quality management systems. For the last three decades, Letran Calamba had significant accomplishments in quality learning and instruction, infrastructure development, research undertakings, environment-related advocacies, and community service, among others. It was granted the ISO 9001:2008 certification in November 2013, several local academic program quality accreditations since 2010, and the National Quality Award modeled after the US Malcolm Baldridge Quality Award in 2015.

Specific to community service, Letran Calamba has managed to implement *Makipamuhay (living in the community)*, a three-day social immersion program for students and school personnel, since year 2000. Letran Calamba, in collaboration with local and international partners, has also developed its community engagement mother program called *Hayuma*, which offers extension and community services in forms of education, disaster risk reduction management, nutrition, livelihood, and public health projects. Letran Calamba is an environmental advocate, promoting environmental protection by implementing practices such as maintaining a waste water treatment facility, proper waste segregation, avoidance of the use of plastics and styrofoams, energy conservation by adapting LED lights and programmable logic circuits (PLC) in controlling air-conditioning units, and 7S implementation—an upgraded 5S.

Through its Graduate School and Professional Services, Letran Calamba has embraced the mission of providing professionals with advanced, innovative, needs-based, and responsible business and management education for continuous improvement, lifelong learning, and integral human development. The school commits itself to nurture and shape its graduate students who are predominantly professionals and holders of key managerial positions in their respective organizations to be responsible managers—that is, by being responsible stewards of God's creation and maintaining a deep sense of affection and empathy to those who belong to the less-privileged and marginalized sectors of the society, to name a few. Letran Calamba became a signatory to the PRME principles in January 19, 2015.

This chapter aims to make sense of the school's advocacy to contribute to responsible management education through relevant courses that deal with social orientation and care for the environment.

Interventions

The Design, Organization, and Execution of the Three Courses on Responsible Management

The Graduate School and Professional Services (GSPS) of Colegio de San Juan de Letran, Calamba, being an outcome-based education (OBE) believer, would like to see its faculty members carry out the very essence and purpose of this undertaking without sacrificing academic freedom in their domain. With this as the guiding principle, each faculty member must be able to provide better approaches and methodologies in the respective courses they handle. They are guided by the identified graduate attributes, course intended learning outcomes (CILOs), and intended learning outcomes (ILOs), in the preparation of the course syllabus. This includes the subject matters/contents; teaching and learning activities;

course assessment; course requirement; course policy; textbook and references, including research journals; and its delivery.

For this study, three graduate courses from three different academic programs were considered, namely: Social Responsibility and Good Governance, Environmental Technology Management, and Transformational Leadership. Social Responsibility and Good Governance is a core course in all the master's-level programs in the graduate school, while the Environmental Technology and Management is a major course under the Master in Management and Master in Management major in Engineering Management, respectively. Transformational Leadership is a core course in all the Doctorate Programs.

Faculty members who were assigned in the aforementioned courses provided an account of each course. In particular, the three courses were characterized in terms of: (a) underlying pedagogies; (b) manner by which the learning activities are facilitated; (c) the learning outcomes and their assessments; and (d) challenges and opportunities for continual enhancement of said courses. Insights and learnings from the courses were also drawn from some of the students of the courses.

The focus of this chapter is on how the three courses contribute to the graduate students' quest to (a) advocate social responsibility, (b) deepen their commitment to care of creation and (c) be guided by the principles of transformational leadership in their respective workplace and communities. These were also attested by the students themselves.

1. **Social Responsibility and Good Governance. Deepening the Professionals' Social Orientation and Community Engagement**

   The course "Social Responsibility and Good Governance" is the core course in five master's-level programs, namely: (1) Master in Business Administration (MBA); (2) Master in Management (MM) major in People Management (MM-PM); (3) MM major in Information Technology Management (MM-ITM); (4) MM major in School Management (MM-SM); and (5) MM major in Engineering Management (MM-EM). Please see Annexure 3.1 for details of the courses.

   The Master in Business Administration (MBA) program provides the students with valuable knowledge about business and all its related aspects, and the opportunity to acquire formal management orientation, integrating the managers' and entrepreneurs' perspectives to the practice of business management. The program plays within an atmosphere conducive to a free exchange of ideas with other executives and business leaders. It aims to develop and sharpen the managers' and entrepreneurs' analytical ability in dissecting business problems and opportunities. Moreover, the decision-making skills of managers and entrepreneurs are strengthened in a multidimensional perspective.

The Social Responsibility and Good Governance course examines the value and trends in engaging stakeholders of a firm to identify new accountability boundaries and establish governance systems, structures, processes and policies to improve the firm's management quality and competitiveness. The course revisits how companies that perform better with regard to these issues can increase shareholder value by, for example, properly managing risks, anticipating regulatory action, or accessing new markets while contributing to the sustainable development of the societies in which they operate.

To provide meaningful outcomes, the Social Responsibility and Good Governance course includes a substantial discussion on ethics, environmental awareness, and so on. It also includes socially responsive in- and off-campus activities through which students are oriented to different social issues that affect the community and the country as well. The emphasis is on how a company should protect its stakeholders in order to build a continuing exchange flow with its resource suppliers, such as employees, customers, suppliers, the community, the government and the shareholders. Students are exposed to different facets of good governance and are required to conceptualize community engagement as final course assessment. These are discussed in class so that students will be able to provide inputs back in their respective organizations.

During the class, each group of students is given a topic for them to deliver a presentation about. They are required to access additional information through web search by looking at the best practices of the top 1,000 corporations who excel in the field. The web search part, however, is not the sole responsibility of the reporting group.

Other students not assigned to the topic are likewise advised to do the same to ensure lively class proceedings. The presentation also includes sharing of their respective organization's best practices and experiences. This will be critiqued by the class for possible improvement if any. With this, the class will be able to provide inputs that can be adapted by the presenter's employer.

The school allows some off-site sessions for each class so that alternative activities can be scheduled. These give time for students to meet, brainstorm, and conduct inspections in the potential engagement sites. The students plan, organize, implement, and evaluate a community-based project. This is an integrative and final project that paves a way to manifest one of the graduate attributes desired—becoming an ethical and responsible citizen of the world by acting prudently and conscientiously on matters' affecting the welfare of others. Other forms of engaging in the community such as working with those affected by calamities are a welcome development.

Sustainability of the project intervention must be emphasized. The students' employer has to be encouraged to contribute and help provide the needed resources in a sustainable manner. More importantly, beneficiaries of the interventions should be educated also in terms of their crucial role in the project intervention, making such project their own and establishing their commitment toward its sustainability.

As an example, students who visited the Home for the Aged for their final project collaborated with students of other classes through the school's graduate school society, and coordinated with doctors, nurses, and pharmaceutical companies for some medicines and food to be served for lunch during the engagement. It is very interesting to note that students were able to apply their learning from other courses they were enrolled in.

In order to process the learnings of the engagement, faculty in charge conducted an evaluation activity immediately after the engagement. During this session, students shared their insights regarding the conducted activity. Likewise, to give students the chance to assess the very activity they themselves made, they were asked to submit an individual reflection paper a week after the engagement.

Table 3.1 *Constructive alignment of the course's learning outcomes with the set graduate attributes*

AR:00-00-FO-86 rev.03 092014

CONSTRUCTIVE ALIGNMENT OF LETRAN GRADUATE ATTRIBUTES (GA), INSTITUTIONAL INTENDED LEARNING OUTCOMES (IILO), AND COURSE INTENDED LEARNING OUTCOMES (CILO)

Course: MAS 073 – Social Responsibility and Good Governance

GRADUATE ATTRIBUTES	IILO	CILO* *After completing this course, students must be able to:*
A *glocally* competent leader	Develop leadership in one's field of study	CILO 1: Practice leadership skills in making ethical decisions and resolving conflict involving the corporation's stakeholders.
A critical thinker	Adopt a multi-level view of the world	CILO 2: Differentiate organizations based on their corporate social responsibility and good governance practices.
A sensible communicator	Articulate arguments clearly and sensibly	CILO 3: Argue on the pros and cons in implementing Corporate Social Responsibility (CSR) in the organization.
A lifelong learner	Engage in research and continuous learning	CILO 4: Critique well- known corporations on the way they implement Corporate Social Responsibility (CSR) to benefit their stakeholders. CILO 5: Analyze the way corporations practice good governance principles as well as implement Corporate Social Responsibility
A reflective steward of God's creation	Show Dominican values in caring for the earth	CILO 6: Design a comprehensive project / program that will have a significant impact in the environment.

1

References: AR:00-00-QF-19
AR:00-00-PW-17;AR:00-00-PW-19;
AR:00-00-PW-26

GSPS Syllabus Format

Since the activity was the final assessment of the course, a rubric that includes planning, participation, record keeping, reflection output, and value of service or initiative was prepared exclusively for this kind of engagement that students were supposed to fill. Table 3.1 shows the constructive alignment of the course's learning outcomes with the set graduate attributes.

2. **Environmental Technology Management: Espousing a Deeper Sense of Responsibility and Accountability for Care of Creations**
The course "Environmental Technology Management" is offered under the Master in Management major in Engineering Management (MM-EM) program. The MM-EM program is designed to enhance the capabilities of engineering faculty members and cadet engineers through updating them on the advances and recent developments in engineering and technology, and by strengthening their comprehension of engineering principles. The program emphasizes the continuity of management- and engineering-related efforts from planning through design to execution. In addition to technical engineering topics, the program provides managerial, business,

marketing, financial, legal, and information system tools for an engineering management career in either the industry or the academic sector. The students will emerge with management and business skills to allow effective performance in directing engineering organizations and in assessing clients and their options from a business and engineering standpoint.

This course introduces the students to various activities in society involving the transformation of material and energy for the benefit of the community. Students are made aware of both the economic and environmental impact of these activities to society. It is one of the more essential courses of the MM-EM. Generally, the course fosters their capacity for a long-range thinking and prepares them to meet the new challenges as they arise. Similarly, it is also expected to enhance students' ability to identify possible mitigation strategies and improve decision-making skills to formulate implementation policies for sustainable environmental management. Correspondingly, the course enables the students to identify opportunities for more efficient use of resources and the prevention of reduction of industrial wastes, and learn the various techniques to achieve these by developing and implementation of effective environmental management system.

This course prepares the students to address ecological and social systems with specific understanding and an ability to make sense of the complex underlying social and ecological context. Students are engaged in dynamic learning strategies through comprehensive presentations—lectures, research and discussions, application-combined approach, case analysis, article review on related and relevant environmental issues, and actual work-based project on a selected firm. Likewise, skills in auditing with regard to environmental management are also introduced and enhanced through actual work project on selected firm. Table 3.2 shows the course framework.

The course is divided into two parts—midterm and final term, with seven weeks per term. Subject matters/topics are included in Annexure 3.2. The learning activities are facilitated through the following: (a) assigning presentation to each student, enhancing their skills in arguments and presentation: Students show their ability to

Table 3.2 Environmental Technology Management course's learning outcomes with the set graduate attributes

AR:00-00-FO-86 rev.03 092014

Colegio de San Juan de Letran-Calamba
Bucal, City of Calamba
4027 Laguna

GRADUATE SCHOOL AND PROFESSIONAL SERVICES

CONSTRUCTIVE ALIGNMENT OF LETRAN GRADUATE ATTRIBUTES (GA), INSTITUTIONAL INTENDED LEARNING OUTCOMES (IILO), AND COURSE INTENDED LEARNING OUTCOMES (CILO)

Course: Environmental Technology Management

GRADUATE ATTRIBUTES	IILO	CILO* After completing this course, students must be able to:
A critical thinker	Adopt a multi-level view of the world	CILO 1: Figure out the new technologies and approaches in environmental issues
		CILO 2: Evaluate the Environmental Management System through the ISO 14001 adaptation
		CILO 3: Apply various management approaches on the issues of the ff: ecological system, material system, atmospheric system, air pollution management issues, water pollution management issues, hazardous waste management issues, pollution prevention
A technically skilled and innovative worker	Exhibit skills in solving real-life problems	CILO 4: Use audit skills characterizing the appropriate solutions on the existing systems
A lifelong learner	Engage in research and continuous learning	
A globally competent leader	Develop leadership in one's field of study	CILO 5: Assess and apply the environmental relevant laws, LLDA/PDEA/DDB in their respective organizations
A reflective steward of God's creation	Show Dominican values in caring for the earth	CILO 6: Administer actual assessment of firm incorporating all the acquired knowledge, skills, and practice utilizing the ISO 14001 criteria.
A sensible communicator	Articulate arguments clearly and sensibly	
An ethical and responsible citizen	Act prudently on matters affecting one's life	

References: AR:00-00-QP-19
AR:00-00-PW-17; AR:00-00-PW-19;   1   GSPS Syllabus Format
AR:00-00-PW-26

create an environment of scholarly conversation through the aid of visual presentations; (b) sharing experiences, knowledge, and insights on every topic: Students will impart their experiential learning in their respective field of expertise, thus collating the needed knowledge of creating an approach and possible application on other industry's way of solving problems and issues; (c) article discussion and comprehension on relevant environmental issues: an article that will reinforce the concepts and help students explore and analyze new ways of addressing environmental challenges; (d) application-combined approach, where students are exposed to industry practices, apply the ISO 14001 to assess industry practices, benchmark against best practices adopted by top companies: a best way of application on learning through exposure to the top companies that will demonstrate a student's ability to learn in another context of environment.

3. **Transformational Leadership: Echoing Responsibility, Accountability, and Sustainability Attributes in the Transformation Process**
The course "Transformational Leadership" is a core course under all the four doctoral programs being offered by the Graduate School. These programs are (1) Doctor of Philosophy in Management (PhD-M); (2) Doctor of Philosophy in People Management (PhD-PM);

(3) Doctor of Philosophy in Information Technology Management (PhD-ITM); and (4) Doctor of Philosophy in School Management (PhD-SM). See Annexure 3.3 for details of the programs.

The PhD-M program is designed to enhance the professional development of students through mentoring, action research, and practical projects, enabling them to make key leadership contributions in their area of expertise. It helps the students appreciate and analyze current management theories, become subject matter experts in various areas of management, develop a leadership style, effectively manage change, and predict future trends in business/enterprise management. The program further aims to equip the students with advanced managerial skills and knowledge needed to address the problems, issues, and challenges arising in a complex organization, both in the private and public sectors. It builds on the theoretical and practical underpinnings of management anchoring on the dynamics of local and global organizations and their corresponding managerial dimensions.

Aside from the philosophy and advanced organization- and management-related courses, the program's major courses cover the concepts, cases, and issues dealing with school legislation and labor laws, strategic human resource management in education, management of curriculum and instruction, social relations in school management, planning and management of school systems, fiscal administration in school management, management of school services, and educational innovation and technology.

Transformational Leadership is defined as the ability to get people aspire for change, to improve, and to be led. It involves assessing associates' motives, satisfying their needs, and valuing them (Northhouse 2001, cited by Hall et.al. 2012). Transformational leaders, on the other hand, focus on followers, motivating them to high levels of performance, and in the process, help followers develop their own leadership potential (Riggio 2009).

The course deals with the examination of various theoretical concepts and a number of encompassing leadership styles, values, and principles characterizing transformational leadership. It informs of and critiques the concept in relation to various organizational contexts. It underscores how leaders and followers raise one another to higher levels of morality and motivation. In particular, it surveys the organizational culture that transformational leadership nurtures, the priorities and concerns it attends, and the rewards it allocates.

It is specifically designed and offered in the doctoral programs as it necessitates a higher-level theoretical grounding, and presentation of constructs that could lead to new discourses in the underlying topics/subject matters. Since the students are engaged in developing new frameworks and models and testing said models through practical research and case studies, this further encourages them to continue venturing in similar research undertakings and at the same time facilitating training on topics that are relevant to their organizations.

The course is anchored predominantly on the four components of transformational leadership, sometimes referred to as 4 Is. These are: (a) idealized influence (II)—the leader serves as an ideal role model for followers; the leader "walks the talk," and is admired for this; (b) inspirational motivation (IM)—transformational leaders have the ability to inspire and motivate followers. Combined these first two Is are what constitute the transformational leader's charisma; (c) individualized consideration (IC)—transformational leaders demonstrate genuine concern for the needs and feelings of followers. This personal attention to each follower is a key element in bringing out their very best efforts; and (d) intellectual stimulation (IS)—the leader challenges followers to be innovative and creative. A common misunderstanding is that transformational leaders are "soft," but the truth is that they constantly challenge followers to higher levels of performance (Northhouse 2001, cited in Hall et al. 2012).

To be able to deliver the course based on its definition and components as mentioned earlier, the course has adopted three student learning outcomes, namely: (1) critically analyze the transformational leadership in both the theoretical and conceptual perspectives; (2) implement and evaluate strategic practices based on various theories, models, and approaches for achieving organizational transformation; and (3) manifest the characteristics of a responsible leader in the workplace, community, and society as a whole. Table 3.3 shows a sample of one of the module course framework.

Table 3.3 Course outline of transformational leadership sub-module

Colegio de San Juan de Letran Calamba
City of Calamba, Laguna, Philippines 4027 · www.letran-calamba.edu.ph · +63(049) 545-5453
Graduate School and Professional Services

DOC 133 (Transformational Leadership)
1st Trimester AY 2015-2016

COURSE OUTLINE

| Module 3 – Responsible Leadership (5 sessions) | Manifest the characteristics of a responsible leader in the workplace, communities, and society as a whole | Describe the characteristics of a responsible leader following a constructivist perspective

Situate responsible leadership in the context of the organization, community, and the society | Leadership for Corporate Sustainability

Leadership for Corporate Social Responsibility

Ethics and Responsible Leadership | Review and Analysis of Case in Point

Writeshop (for the final paper) | Case Study Paper

Dialectical Paper on Transformational Leadership: Echoing Responsibility, Accountability, and Sustainability of the Organizational Transformation Process (Equivalent to Final Exam) |

GRADUATE SCHOOL AND PROFESSIONAL SERVICES
E-mail: gsps@letran-calamba.edu.ph; letrancalamba_gs@yahoo.com
Tel. No: +63(049) 545-5453 local 4007
Fax: +63(049) 545-4751 (ATTN: Graduate School and Professional Services)

To effectively address the stated outcomes, this course is delivered in three modules. These are: (a) transformational leadership: the conceptual bases and components; (b) transforming the organization: key leadership models; and (c) responsible leadership. Please see Annexure 3.4 for details of each module.

Anchoring on the aforementioned conceptual premises about responsible leadership, students were tasked to prepare a dialectical paper cum literature review of how transformational leadership is echoed within the domains of responsibility, accountability, and sustainability attributes of the organizational transformation process. Among others, and as an additional theoretical paradigm, students were also guided by the core tenets of the responsibility mind-set and new leadership styles authored by Bettignies (2014).

As one of the major assessment tasks of this module, the final research paper of the students served as an opportunity for them to: (a) identify the research gaps based on the literature reviewed; (b) reiterate the scope, pedagogy, and theoretical and conceptual underpinnings of transformational leadership (what and how?) in an integrative and synthesized perspective; (c) identify and explain the parameters used in describing the attributes of transformational leadership; (d) identify various sources of data/information as bases for developing models/frameworks for echoing responsibility, accountability, and sustainability attributes; and

(e) develop framework/model for echoing the three attributes and establish their respective indicators and outcomes.

The final paper enabled them to critically dissect related literatures, and deduce theoretical, conceptual, and pragmatic models to best explain the tenets of sustainability, accountability, and responsibility of the individual, and eventually model their own paradigm as contribution to the body of knowledge of said course. Here, the students were able to relate the cases representing different industries to the theoretical and conceptual paradigms. In addition, students were challenged to apply the perspectives in their respective organizations.

It is believed that the course learning outcome 3 (manifest the characteristics of a responsible leader in the workplace, community, and society as a whole) may be initially realized upon mainstreaming in the concepts, practices, and principles of responsible leadership. The indicators and outcomes as formulated through the research project, once used in the actual workplace, may contribute to the manifestation of characteristics of responsible leadership as the students (who are predominantly handling managerial positions) would be guided in facilitating the organizational transformation processes.

Challenges and Outcomes

Challenges

The course on social responsibility tends to have bias toward doing community outreach and giving back to society. The challenge for instructors is how to reorient students to a broader notion of responsibility—not just as a community outreach program but rather as an entry point to further appreciate a bigger picture about the other problems and issues that beset a society. With such a challenge, the intended learning outcomes and subject matter should be carefully identified and matched.

For the course Transformation Leadership, the challenge is to get students to apply the underlying theories and concepts in their respective workplaces. This could be in the form of process mapping, where one can situate a particular process in their company where transformation is necessary, or do a social audit of their respective organizations to determine where are they situated in the corporate social responsibility (CSR) pyramid. Discourses among various perspectives are helpful. With the introduction of sustainable development goals (SDGs), this could serve as a very rich source of arguments as they relate to social responsibility, corporate sustainability, and environmental consciousness, and call for action.

In the process of teaching the course Environmental Technology Management, on the other hand, most of the students already know about auditing as they are exposed to ISO 14001 (Environmental Management System). However, the real essence of its implications was not clear. By including the process of environmental impact assessment, students could actively participate in the compliance and certification process in their respective organizations. It is a challenge to help them realize the essence of environment management systems and become more conscious of their responsibility in managing waste materials, especially in the manufacturing setting. Most of the students have inadequate understanding of the waste water treatment operation. In order to reinforce the learning process, students need to be exposed to actual waste water treatment facility, which could be an opportunity for them to clarify some related concepts as applied in the field from those technical people who are operating the facility.

Outcome

There were 21 master's-level students who took the course Social Responsibility and Good Governance and eight doctorate students for the course Transformational Leadership. They are largely employed while attending the course. These two courses were taken during the first trimester of academic year 2015 to 2016. The Environmental Technology and Management, on the other hand, was taken by 11 master's-level students during the second trimester of academic year 2014 to 2015. The students' learnings and insights for Social Responsibility and Good Governance and Transformational Leadership were taken from the narratives that were attached to the final papers of the students. One hundred percent of the students had submitted the said narratives. For Environmental Technology and Management, the feedback came from the qualitative evaluation of student as requested by its professor. Annexure 3.5 details the comments of students who gave feedback, specifically their account of their experience, learnings, and insights, either about the specific course activities or the overall delivery of the course in general. Please see Annexure 3.5 for details of the specific comments.

With respect to the course on Social Responsibility and Good Governance, students appear to have appreciated the experience of volunteering. They express this with terms such as "blessed" and "thankful." They were able to make a difference to others, be a blessing to others, and become more aware of the plight of less fortunate. They said they would encourage their companies to be socially responsible. In respect to the course on Environmental Technology Management, students appreciated the importance given to being a responsible citizen (preventing harmful effects on environment) while being conscientious about operational efficiencies. They appreciated the practice given in analyzing environmental problems and making policies/systems to address them, and the opportunity to apply environmental management to their own organizations. In the course on Transformational Leadership, comments were about the interactive, enlightening discussions, about leaders as agents of change. They felt that transformational leadership was necessary in the government. For the enhancement of the course, students themselves recommended to include role-playing, inviting resource persons who are currently engaged and active in the field or topic they would be speaking about, and more case studies with Asian flavor.

Conclusions

The students' reflections about their experience and learnings from the courses are indication that indeed these courses are life-changing and inspiring them further to continuously seek additional knowledge and wisdom, and apply them in the real world. While there are definitely challenges and constraints that they may encounter, still, the experience would hopefully matter still, as they advocate that organizations move toward being socially responsible and ethical citizens, manifesting deep affection for the poor and marginalized ones, and being reflective stewards of God's creation.

In final analysis, it is of utmost concern, if not at all, for graduate education to deliver the best to its students, through ways in which courses are delivered by the faculty themselves, the prevailing environment that dictates the conduciveness of the learning process, and ultimately, the realization of learning by making knowledge work in diverse workplaces and communities where they belong. Since the students of the graduate school are mostly professionals, the three courses as mentioned prepare them to become responsible managers or employees, champions of the environment in their workplaces, and catalysts in their respective organizations by bringing about the transformation in terms of setting organizational culture of the companies with respect to what the society expects from them.

This chapter started with a mention of the 21st-century challenges facing the higher education institutions in bringing about significant impact and/or contribution to addressing the increasing population of the poor and marginalized sectors of the society, and the adverse effect of climate change. In the advent of the new sustainable development paradigm as outlined in the SDGs, a question revolves on how higher educational institutions can effectively become a core stakeholder for achieving the set goals. The Graduate School of Letran Calamba introduced responsible management education and, in particular, committed to nurturing the professionals in social orientation and care of creation through the three courses. The underlying stories, accounts of students' learnings and insights, and faculty experience in teaching the courses combined, are indeed a good start but still wanting for more. Nevertheless, the journey at least has begun, and, in the process, the improvement in the design, delivery, and evaluation of responsible management education in the graduate school would become a continuing saga.

Bibliography

Borecka, M. 2014. Developing the Next Generation of Responsible Leaders: Empirical Insights and Recommendations for Organizations, University of St. Gallen, School of Management, Economics, Law, Social Sciences and International Affairs, Zurich, Germany.

Bettignies, H. C. 2014. "The Five Dimensions of Responsible Leadership," http://knowledge.insead.edu/responsibility/the-five-dimensions-of-responsible-leadership-3685#Duiujirx2KFBpZ1E.99

Balba, A. K., E. L. M. Mamino, and M. G. Reyes. 2015. Transformational Leadership: Echoing Responsibility, Accountability, and Sustainability

Attributes in the Transformation Process. A Final Research Paper for the Course DOC 133—Transformational Leadership, 1st Trimester, A.Y. 2015–2016, Graduate School and Professional Services, Colegio de San Juan de Letran, Calamba, Philippines.

Caymo, M. C, de los Santos, M. M., Padayao, P. M. T, and Viloria, D. D. 2015. Transformational Leadership: Echoing Responsibility, Accountability, and Sustainability Attributes in the Transformation Process. A Final Research Paper for the Course DOC 133—Transformational Leadership, 1st Trimester, A.Y. 2015–2016, Graduate School and Professional Services, Colegio de San Juan de Letran, Calamba, Philippines.

Graduate School and Professional Services, 2015. Social Responsibility and Good Governance Compilation of Reports, Course's Final Activity Documentation, and Reflection Papers, 1st Trimester, A.Y. 2015–2016, Colegio de San Juan De Letran Calamba, Philippines.

Hall, J., S. Johnson, A. Wysochi, and K. Kepner, K. 2012. Transformational Leadership: The transformation of Managers and Associates. In http://edis.ifas.ufl.edu, University of Florida, USA.

Morandarte, M. C. 2015. Social Responsibility and Good Governance Course Syllabus, 1st Trimester AY 2015–2016, Graduate School and Professional Services, Colegio de San Juan de Letran Calamba, Philippines.

Northhouse, P. G. 2001. Leadership: Theory and Practice. Sage Publications.

Principles for Responsible Management Education. 2015. Participant Guide, 2015 Global Forum for Responsible Management Education-6th PRME Assembly, June 23–24, 2015. New York City.

Riggio, R. E. 2009. Are You a Transformational Leader?, In Psychology Today. com, retrieved July 25, 2005.

Robles, R. 2014. Environmental Technology and Management, 1st Trimester AY 2014–2015, Graduate School and Professional Services, Colegio de San Juan de Letran Calamba, Philippines.

Internet Sources

www.philippine-history.org/edsa-people-power-revolution.htm, retrieved 23 August 2016

www.asj.upd.edu.ph/mediabox/archive/ASJ-39-1-2-2003/gonzalez.pdf, retrieved August 23, 2016

Annexure 3.1

Brief Details of the Master's-Level Program

The Master of Management major in People Management is designed to help students deepen their human resource subject matter expertise, and strengthen their ability to think beyond functional boundaries, positioning themselves to become an important partner in developing and implementing workplace strategies that deliver business results. The program aims to enhance the students' proficiency in using human resource management technologies to be able to respond to the vast changing organization environment, apply knowledge in core areas such as compensation (including rewards and recognition), labor management relations, talent management, strategic human resource planning (i.e., strategic staffing, talent acquisition), performance management, and organizational capability development, among others. The program also engages the students in developing critical thinking ability needed to formulate, design, and implement human resource development programs.

The Master in Management major in Information Technology Management (MM-ITM) program provides the students an opportunity to explore the future of advanced and cutting-edge technologies that facilitate the flow of information and communications in an organization and the corresponding management processes at an advanced level. It is designed to facilitate advanced learnings on the utilization and evaluation of information technology (IT) toward meeting changing customer needs and market; on how to weigh the costs/benefits of IT decisions; analyzing and evaluating the effects of IT change on organization; how to help people adopt to change; and how to explore common problems of management and organization, and their relationship to IT.

The Master in Management major in School Management (MM-SM) program is designed for teachers, school administrators, entrepreneurs, and policy makers who are interested in improving their management capabilities, especially in school or any learning institution. It is geared toward equipping the students with the knowledge, attitudes, and skills in the attainment of the desired goals of an institution, namely academic excellence, quality research, and community extension. The program provides the environment conducive to the development and enhancement of a practitioner's educational leadership and management and critical understanding of the complexities of educational organizations. It dwells on the theoretical and practical learning perspectives that are reflective and relevant to concerned stakeholders' educational setting. The program explores on concepts, cases, and issues dealing with the philosophies of education, educational management and administration, comparative analysis of school management in global and cross-cultural contexts, academic policy and strategy formulation, current trends and challenges in education, and other academic/learning institution–related management processes.

Annexure 3.2

Course content of Environmental Technology Management (Source: Robles 2014):

Ecological System/Material System/Atmospheric System—wherein students are exposed on the theoretical discussion on the ecology, on the material system and atmospheric system which will set the tone on the course context of approaching the environmental issues through technologies and systems enhancement.

Air Pollution Management Issues—tackles not only the theoretical discussion on greenhouse effect, global warming, acid rain, indoor air quality among others but also the air pollution control equipment. Techniques used to control gaseous emissions are also being discussed.

Waste Pollution Management Issues—converses the issues hounding the organization and community addressing accordingly. Ditto, the waste water treatment facility in the organization is being explained to make an enhanced contribution to the society.

Solid and Radioactive Waste Management Issues—types of waste are being discussed in the categories residential, commercial, and industrial. Each category's type of waste has key separate process of managing the waste. Local government units (LGUs) and organization have obligations to dispose the waste accordingly.

Hazardous Waste Management Issues—the related topics focus on types of hazards and their required disposal. Students are reminded on the strict implementation of proper disposal as this will be having corresponding actions and penalties from the relevant agencies.

Pollution Prevention—a vital topic in the students exploration of the use of 3Rs (Reuse, Reduce, and Recycle) in their respective organizations. One topic that students can quickly adapt to their entity is the application of 3Rs wherein a comprehensive process mapping will certainly give strategies to solve preventing pollution at their sphere of controls.

ISO 14001—it being the heart of the course is delivered as a management tool to have a better control of EMS (Environmental Management System). Utilizing the criteria of ISO 14001, a thorough discussion on each element is done to ensure that the application will be relevant to whatever organization the student belongs. Similarly, auditing skills are being taught and facilitated to examine the holistic view of the possible solutions on the issues encountered.

Risk Related Topics—concentrates on hazard identification with the needed management and control. It is very essential on the student to learn on its identification and have corresponding formulated mitigation.

LLDA—or Laguna Lake Development Authority, a key learning in the vicinity of most of the students where compliance of waste water management with the specified parameters is required by said regulatory body. Similarly, one profession as PCO (Pollution Control Officer) is explained as regards the associated duties and responsibilities. It also becomes a possible employment career path for the students.

Recent Developments—students are exposed to the recent developments as regards to addressing environmental issues.

New Technologies and Approaches—learnings are focused on the new technologies such as bioremediation, soil vapor extraction, and biofiltration, among others.

Firm Assessment—ultimately, this exposes the students into real applications of the learning wherein a firm assessment is assigned incorporating the use of ISO14001 criteria. Consequently, students hone their skills in ISO 14001 auditing while gathering best practices which can be applied in their respective organizations.

Annexure 3.3

Description of Doctoral Programs

The Doctor of Philosophy major in People Management (PhD-PM) program is designed to prepare students to lead, consult, or teach in the field of human resources within a complex and global business environment. It helps in developing human resource practitioners' skills in analyzing the relationship between human resource functions and corporate/business strategy, with the end goal of providing appropriate intervention toward sustained human resource management. The program further prepares the students to be actively involved in exploring and creating practical solutions to human resource–related problems, contributing to the formulation of best alternative and options for decision-making. It equips the students with critical thinking skills and innovative approaches in leading and managing the organization's human assets.

The Doctor of Philosophy major in Information Technology Management (PhD-ITM) program is designed for students who are interested in pursuing advanced study of business and information technology management. It aims to enhance the students' articulation of how IT changes the way businesses operate and the dynamics of managing the IT resources and processes as anchored on various IT architecture and infrastructure frameworks and models. The program deals with interdisciplinary study in management and information systems and focuses on theory and practice, the dimensions of organizations, and the associated IT leadership and governance. Graduates will develop the advanced leadership and management skills needed in the business world to provide innovative, real-world solutions to complex IT issues.

The Doctor of Philosophy major in School Management is an advanced program that aims to develop school managers who are responsive to the global and national needs for quality research and development. It will help a student master a core of professional and theoretical knowledge and demonstrate skills in applied research and the practice of leadership. Through the promotion of advanced studies, practicum, and research, school managers are guided in enriching their leadership capabilities, thus becoming more responsive to the challenges of socially transforming schools/learning institutions and school systems.

Annexure 3.4

Modules of the Course on Transformational Leadership

Module 1. Transformation Leadership: The Conceptual Bases and Components: This module is aligned to student learning outcome 1. At the end of this module, students should be able to explain the concept behind the transformational leadership. This module covers the conceptual paradigm of transformational leadership, the four factors to transformational leadership, and qualities of a transformational leader. Topics are facilitated and delivered through personal reflection, group discussion, and persona analysis (transformational leadership in action). Students' performance is assessed through the reflection output (with rubrics), and case study on transformational leadership personified.

Module 2. Transforming the Organization: Key Leadership Models: This module corresponds to student learning outcome 2. Through this module, students are given the opportunity to (a) identify the different leadership styles and their functions in the transformation process; (b) describe the various philosophical thoughts in transformation leadership as applied in organization; and (c) analyze and evaluate the role of the strategic leader in planning and guiding the change process in organization. The key topics discussed are: (a) leadership styles and their functions in the transformation process; (b) leading change in the organization: guiding principles and critical thoughts; (c) leadership strategies and tactics; (d) impact of transformational leaders in organization; and (e) issues and challenges in leading the organization toward change. Learning activities are facilitated through review and analysis of case in point, theoretical mapping, and literature review on transforming the organization through efficacy of leadership styles. Here, the students' performance is assessed in terms of ratings in case study paper, discourse analysis (written and oral), and research paper (which is equivalent to one major exam).

Module 3. Responsible Leadership: This module specifically addresses student outcome 3. Here, students are able to describe the characteristics of a responsible leader through a constructivist perspective. Also, they are able to situate responsible leadership as concept and paradigm in the context of the organization, community, and the society. Leadership is discussed and analyzed within the frames of corporate sustainability, CSR, and ethics and responsibility. Cases drawn from industry accounts are examined and analyzed using dialectics as an approach. Four meetings are allocated for discussion and writeshop to prepare the final research paper on echoing responsibility, accountability, and sustainability of the organizational transformation process. The writeshop is facilitated, normally in two to three meetings, in which the students are given the opportunity to use the class hours to write their papers. Faculty in charge is also present to facilitate both cliniquing and critiquing processes. Cliniquing is a process by which the students ask for clarification on certain issues/parts of the research paper. Here, there is a reinforcement being done by the faculty-in-charge, reiterating the need to incorporate the knowledge base gained from the course, among others. In critiquing, students show the draft of the research paper and the faculty-in-charge facilitates a research conference to provide his or her comments/suggestions. In essence, students become well guided and ensure that the paper preparation is on the right track prior to the presentation.

Responsible Leadership and Management and the Organizational Transformation Process: Leadership, in this course, is treated as a new paradigm, looking at the perspective of organizational transformation as the leader echoes responsibility, accountability, and sustainability attributes at the individual, organizational, and community levels. Students are engaged in intellectual discourse, dissecting new ways of understanding the phenomenon behind the transformation process, aimed at constructing new theories that best explain such a phenomenon. In the context of the objective of this case study, one of the authors (Maningas) put more emphasis on module 3. Mark and Pless (2006b) as cited in Borecka (2014) define responsible leadership as "a social-relational phenomenon," which occurs in social processes of interaction with those who affect or are affected by leadership, it aims to build and sustain good, trustful, and sustainable relationships with all relevant stakeholders within an organization and outside its borders unlike the prevailing literature which has usually focused on the relationship between leaders and followers in the organization and has defined followers as subordinates. Responsible leaders, on the other hand, are defined as those who bring together different people to follow a shared and morally sound vision for which they need moral character and relational qualities. Accordingly, by building and cultivating sustainable relationships with internal and external stakeholders, responsible leaders achieve mutually shared objectives based on the vision of the business as a force of good for the many, and not just few (shareholders, managers, etc.) (cited by Borecka 2014). This module is introduced as an additional topic in Transformational Leadership, as this is considered as one of its key attributes. Responsible leadership is beyond the leader–follower dictum. As such, in facilitating the organizational transformation to effectively achieve set goals or targets, leaders must embrace the responsible leadership frame of thoughts, looking at the effects of the transformation to the individuals, the organizations, and the society as a whole.

Annexure 3.5

Qualitative Feedback on Each Course

Feedback About Course on Social Responsibility and Good Governance

"The activity made me thankful. It made me blessed. ..... gave me an opportunity to extend myself for others. I know they will eventually forget about us but the most important thing is that I made them happy...... I know I made a difference, and my goal now is to be a catalyst."

"I would also encourage my present employer to partake in social responsibility, not as an obligation by as a way of sharing and thanksgiving to all the profit it is receiving. "

"During the class discussions and with ... (the teacher's) help, I actually understand how important CSR is in an organization, and on how it directly affects the lives of their employees, and the people who are not part of the organization, as well. .... I can apply ... to give others the opportunity to grow, and also to inspire other people to do right and to help those who are in need"

"In my own capacity, I will continuously help and support our less fortunate people to the best way that I can do. In our organization, I will strongly suggest to sustain current CSR activities and include it in the key performance indicators (KPIs) of the organization, so we can monitor the progress."

"I feel that volunteering only betters yourself, and it helps others. It is a great way to support a community as well as meet new people, and to help out others."

"The CSR class opened my eyes, my heart, and my hand to those less fortunate people around me. I just hope that I could be able to live with the principle of trying to be the blessing to the others"

"I remember when... (the teacher) ... told us that in order for us to understand what really CSR is, we need to be with the people and try to feel what they need."

"Thank you CSR for the experience and .... to me to bring more for the society"

"After visiting the old age home, I was reminded even more to be thankful for what I have"

"It's was an awakening experience especially to me as a young professional."

"This experience of visiting the elderly reminds me of how big a small gesture can have on people who least expect it. And that's where they get their strength, living the life with surprises."

Feedback on Environmental Technology Management

"ETM (Environmental Technology Management) open our eyes on the implementation not only on the operations aspect but on the environmental management using technological approaches and system"

"The course not just equipped us with the theoretical aspect but with the applications relevant to our organization"

"It gave us a sense of responsible citizen while conscientious in the operations or process that we are operating"

"Continue exploring efficient operations through the use of 3Rs in my section"

"Environmental Technology Management explores environmental problems, issues or concerns brought by organizational activities of different industries that require immediate and effective solutions to eliminate or mitigate

risk to protect all living things on earth. The course teaches how to dwell on specific environmental issues by providing case analysis and true to life scenarios. With these, students have been able to practice analyzing environmental problems or situations enabling them to formulate ideas, best strategies, and decisions to protect environment. Some of the common issues in the organization that can affect the environment are air emissions, wastewater discharges such as oils and grease, handling and disposal of hazardous chemicals, and disposal of solid wastes. These issues may require necessary controls to prevent harmful effects to the environment. Thus, the organization should set specific objectives, targets, and programs to manage the environment"

"Our organization, B/E Aerospace B.V Philippines, an organization which provides world class aircraft interior products to customers are currently implementing policies and procedures to meet at least the minimum requirement of ISO14001 certification. ISO14001 sets out the criteria for an effective Environmental Management System. Aiming to acquire the certification, we are one to support EHS programs by strictly following environmental policies and procedures, by giving suggestions to improve processes which contribute to environmental aspects, and by imparting knowledge to the EHS committee. We place departmental objectives to support plant wide OTP's by initiating programs such as the 3Rs—reduce, reuse, and recycle of paper wastes and packaging materials, and segregation of biodegradable and non-biodegradable wastes. We have set a limit for our energy usage by monitoring electricity and water. We implement Preventive Maintenance of machines to ensure tolerable dust particles are obtained. We also monitor the volume of our solid wastes and ensure that these are properly disposed. Furthermore, part of our KPI (key performance index) that all new and regular employees, visitors, and contractors have been trained or oriented about the plant's EHS policies and programs. This is our advocacy that we are responsible and committed for the attainment of sustainable and effective Environmental Management System."

Feedback on Transformational Leadership

"Packaging the course topics into modularized learning blocks is a great idea. Personally, I think it provided the students a better guidance in the flow of the discussion and learning process from start to end. We started from the theoretical groundings and concept discussions of transformational leadership.

The leveling up to the global stage of corporate sustainability, where responsible, accountable, and sustainable leadership is situated has provided a wider perspective of leadership role in the global arena. The contents of the discussion were very enlightening, very informative, and personally, this is very helpful to me since I am currently performing leadership role in our company's pursuit for sustainable business (inclusion of environment in our business targets and outcomes)."

"Transformational leadership is a personal and organizational process. Transformational leadership entails transformation from the leader himself then extended to his organization directed toward human well-being, economic growth, and environmental sustainability. Leaders, no matter the size of his/her organization is challenged to echo responsibility, accountability, and sustainability. This course has led me to insights to conduct future research in this topic."

"I have taken a lot of leadership training programs but it was my first time to see leadership from a different light—leadership as the agent of change. Managing change is the very heart of transformational leadership. There could be a lot of leadership styles a leader may possess, whose applicability depends on the challenges he faces, but what makes the transformational type different is its ability to handle transformation turnarounds while keeping the organization from getting left behind.... By gradually increasing awareness of the concept of responsible leadership and actually engaging it in their current processes is indeed a test of transformational leadership in itself."

"Recognizing that transformational leadership is what is needed most in government, most political leaders themselves need to transform themselves first before even dreaming of transforming society."

"Responsible leadership is not something to be argued about, rather it must be put into practice and maintaining accountability and the passion to sustain it. I agree that ethics is the heart of leadership. Being a leader particularly echoing transformational leadership resounds the melody of responsibility, accountability, and sustainability among the members of the organization, and being echoed to a wider scope not only on individual level but also to organizational and global levels. I think every academic institutional leaders must internalize transformational leadership qualities at all times."

"In this course, I was confronted by the realization that there is still more to know, more to learn, more to comprehend and because I made the decision

to accept the challenge, I am confident to say, I am a lot better leader now—a transformative leader."

"What made the course instructive and entertaining was the interactive discussions of the class as a group. I learned a lot from the sharing and intelligent arguments. That we had different interpretations and views on various issues only made the exchange of ideas lively and inspiring."

CHAPTER 4

The Centre for Corporate Sustainability and Innovations, Hang Seng Management College, Hong Kong

Shirley Mo-Ching Yeung

Director, Centre for Corporate Sustainability and Innovations (CCSI), Hang Seng Management College, Hong Kong

Background

There has been an increasing demand for sustainability in recent decades, especially under pressure from global warming, the oil crisis and the search for renewable energy. Hence, all sectors are exploring methods for sustainable growth. The higher education (HE) sector is exploring the development of a curriculum that promotes sustainability mind-set among students, employers, institutions, and the community.

Recently, the United Nations Educational, Scientific and Cultural Organization (UNESCO), the United Nations (UN) Global Compact (UNGC), and the UN Principles for Responsible Management Education (PRME) have promoted the concept of Education for Sustainable Development (ESD). According to UNESCO, ESD is "a process of learning how to make decisions that consider the long-term future of the economy, ecology and equity of all communities" (UNESCO 2004 in Djordjevic and Cotton 2011). At an institutional level, ESD involves campus changes, curriculum development, and pedagogic reform. Some examples include enhancing the sustainability content of courses, inclusion of a deeper reflection element, and campaigns to change staff and students' use of energy/paper.

Yeung (2011) mentioned that with the growing importance of national/international validation, adherence to external standards—such as that of the Quality Assurance Department (Malaysian Ministry of Higher Education, 2008)—is becoming necessary for educational institutions. Some of these standards require educators to align program objectives and course learning outcomes to sustainable development (Yeung, 2011). This could require changes in teachers' beliefs and assumptions about learning (Bajunid 2014). Education policies must support continual professional development of scholars, teachers, and industry practitioners to better understand the linkage between sustainable development and responsible management in various industries.

New competencies for a sustainability mind-set—such as systemic thinking, creativity, collaboration—need to be inculcated among students. However, these competencies are often not inculcated for the following reasons: (a) Educators assume that such abilities are already present in the student or faculty body; (b) educators in HE settings do not know that such competencies are important; (c) educators know such competencies are important but are not provided training in such methodology, or (d) the student numbers are large. This opens an improvement area in HE for educators/lecturers with more solid experience in utilizing different approaches to the traditional didactic methods.

In the Asia Pacific region and elsewhere, there is need for collaboration with other stakeholders to make more progress towards education for Sustainable Development (Ryan and Tilbury, 2013). Such partnerships could help develop new models of education for sustainable development.

HE in Hong Kong

According to Hong Kong government's Manpower Project Report 2018, the top three economic sectors anticipated to grow the fastest in terms of manpower requirements during the period from 2010 to 2018 are *financial services* (at an average annual rate of 2.5 percent), *construction* (1.9

percent), and *information and communications* (1.9 percent). The manpower requirements of six industries in Hong Kong—education services, medical services, testing and certification services, environmental industries, innovation and technology, and cultural and creative industries—were expected to grow between 1.6 to 4.4 percent. According to the report on educational services, training to business firms and continuing education to improve productivity were expected to gain in importance. There was a recognition that the quality of education had to be promote awareness about Sustainable Development (SD).

During the First Forum on Sustainable Development in Higher Education, Hong Kong, 2015, Hong Kong Council for Accreditation of Academic and Vocational Qualifications (HKCAAVQ) mentioned that ensuring relevant, high quality education required (a) partnerships and quality assurance; (b) modification of the programs to equip students with the values, knowledge, and skills for SD; and (c) use of real-life situations as case studies, service learning, and social engagement to help students learn ways of tackling new problems. There was need to review course relevance, course structures, and appropriateness to local culture.

This chapter describes the role played by the Centre of Corporate Sustainability and Innovations (CCSI)—situated in a private tertiary education institution called Hang Seng Management College (HSMC)—in responding to the concern for SD and accomplishing the vision, mission, and strategic goals of the parent institutions through partnerships.

The Institution

Hang Seng School of Commerce (HSSC) was founded in 1980 and restructured into HSMC, a new nonprofit private university registered under the Post-Secondary Colleges Ordinance (Cap 320) to offer bachelor's and higher degree programs in diversified disciplines. Presently, HSMC has five schools (Business, Communication, Decision Sciences, Humanities and Social Science, and Translation) with 14 undergraduate programs in business administration, corporate governance, financial analysis, management, journalism, and communication, and a master's degree program in translation.

The vision of HSMC is to be a leading private university, recognized for excellence in teaching, learning, and research, especially in the areas of business and management. HSMC desires to contribute positively to the economic, social, and environmental conditions of the community and to the quality of life of its staff and their families, as well as the local community and society at large. It aims to achieve this by providing quality business- and management-related programs to students to meet the job market needs with social responsibility (SR) and an ethical mind-set. The 10 strategic goals of CCSI were to create value for its stakeholders—students, the academic and the nonacademic community (see Annexure 4.1 for the strategic goals).

HSMC created the CCSI in March 2015 to lead the self-financed higher educational institutions and industries in building a platform for dialogue on social responsibility (SR), sustainability and innovations. The vision of the Centre is to cocreate a platform for services/products related to SR, sustainability and innovation. The Centre's mission is to seek ways to engage stakeholders in the practice of SR, sustainability and innovation.

The CCSI aims to align the strategic plan of the parent institution with emergent international and national trends in sustainable development (SD) and social responsibility. It aims to increase awareness among educators, industry practitioners, the government, and NGOs about sustainable development and social responsibility through a variety of programs conducted in partnership with other international and national agencies.

Objectives of CCSI

1. Provide stakeholders with the competencies and mindset for social responsibility and sustainable development.
2. Provide stakeholders with opportunities to appreciate and apply knowledge of social responsibility and sustainable development to make a better world.
3. Conduct and report on events/activities that address the values of UN Global Compact and the Principles for Responsible Management Education (PRME)

Interventions at CCSI

Initiatives of CCSI

CCSI organized the First Forum on Sustainable Development in Higher Education on July 21, 2015. This was followed by a series of follow-up events on sustainable development for business and community development. The events attracted speakers from intergovernmental organizations, for example, United Nations, PRME, and scholars and industry practitioners from the United States, Israel, Ukraine, and Malaysia. These events created a platform for academia, practitioners, intergovernmental organizations, and the government to discuss new approaches to sustainable development and to responsible management education. There were also action-based seminars to explore solutions to sustainability challenges. There was agreement that the sustainability mind-set is necessary and must be integrated into education.

CCSI realized the importance of building partnerships with diverse organizations to design and deliver conferences and workshops on responsible management and sustainable development. The programs increased awareness about responsible management and sustainable development among executives, teachers and students. PRME and UNGC became key partners in the international colloquium and subsequent activities of CCSI, to promote an sustainable development (SD) mind-set, entrepreneurial spirit, and innovations.

According to the PRME/UNGC, the new emphasis on sustainability requires changes in corporate practices: a focus away from philanthropic, compliance-driven, reactive orientation toward one that embeds sustainability in business decisions. Effecting such a change requires dialoguing with public officials, other leading companies, and relevant trade and industry associations on critical sustainability issues. It requires creating unique opportunity for engagement with public policy on responsible management.

A few of the Centre's salient events/activities to promote the sustainability mind-set are detailed below:

Modification of HSMC programs. The Centre has helped integrate the United Nation's Sustainable Development Goals (SDGs) into the

Operations Management (OM) module of the college's undergraduate and postgraduate programs. The module outline, assignments, assessment rubrics, and teaching materials will be updated to reflect the importance of the SDGs.

The module will include a discussion of the following issues: (a) the Global Compact and PRME principles; (b) the potential target community to be served; (c) the economic and social benefits to be maximized; (d) changing demographics and the new products/services that could meet changing needs; (e) supportive technological, political and legal changes required to promote responsible production and consumption of these products/services; (f) the need for partnership with downstream and upstream organizations to improve the quality of new products/services/processes, and the quality of life for stakeholders.

Career Fairs and Youth Leadership Camps. With the support of United Nations Office for South-South Cooperation (UNOSSC), the CCSI and Harvard University jointly conducted the Harvard HPAIR Career Fair on August 22, 2016, in Hong Kong Science Park. The Harvard HPAIR Career Fair is a pivotal event for professional networking between the student delegates and the corporate world. It aims to provide a platform for delegates to explore their career prospects through engagement with corporations of various industries. Twenty to 30 world-renowned companies were invited to interact with 550 delegates of a wide range of disciplines at the event.

The Career Fair provided a platform for delegates from over 60 countries to (a) understand more about responsible management and sustainable development; (c) broaden their perspective on issues related to sustainable enterprises; and (d) discuss career challenges and trends across the international landscape. This activity created a valuable exchange platform and awareness about the need for leaders with an SD mind-set for meeting challenges in the future. During the fair, the concept of "Sustainable Development Mindset for Human-Centred Operations" was shared with participants. The three-hour event on SD mind-set attracted enthusiastic responses from the audience. The delegates recognized CCSI's goals and expressed their interests in CCSI's future activities.

With the support of UNOSSC, CCSI also organized "Sustainability Youth Leadership Camp," to promote and implement SD mind-set and increase international exposure for youth participants in November 2016.

In 2015, CCSI identified opportunities to work with local, regional, and global partners to cocreate a series of activities related to responsible management, sustainable development and developing innovations for society. Annexure 4.2 details CCSI's key activities to promote responsible management and sustainability. The impact of these activities can be demonstrated from the positive feedback of participants and social media coverage of CCSI's affiliates, UNPRME and UNOSSC. Strategic partners and social networks have strengthened the vision, mission statement and objectives of CCSI.

Challenges and Outcomes

According to the Education 2030 Framework of Action, the Incheon Declaration in May 2015, policy formulation to ensure accountability is crucial. The challenges that CCSI has to face are to do with facilitating dialogue with existing and potential partners on policy making, knowledge sharing, and setting mutually agreed standards for monitoring progress toward the targets mentioned in the UNSDGs. Of interest is the SD goal 4 "Quality of Education" target 4.4—which is to substantially increase the number of youth and adults who have relevant skills, including technical and vocational skills, for employment and entrepreneurship by 2030—and 4.7—which is to ensure that all learners acquire the knowledge and skills needed to promote SD by 2030.

In its short tenure since 2015, the Centre was able to conduct several conferences and seminars on SD with government funding. Members of the CCSI have also presented papers at several international conferences on sustainability, Six Sigma, and competitiveness. They mentored students to write stories on SD for UN Flourish and also provided training in developing videos on quality management, CSR, and sustainability. The Centre has also published books on entrepreneurial transformation and corporate sustainability. It is helping HSMC modify its undergraduate and graduate programs to include a discussion on responsible management and sustainable development. The outcomes of CCSI's activities are mentioned in Annexure 4.3.

Conclusion

This chapter described the initiatives of CCSI to promote a dialogue on sustainability among students and other stakeholders of HSMC. Globalized skills and a mind-set of SD can be developed via ongoing dialogue with different stakeholders. This dialogue can result in conferences, workshops, and research that enhance awareness about SD and how it can be integrated into the curriculum of business schools.

It is time for educators and policy makers to think about ways to build a global platform that would develop policies and incentives supportive of sustainable development and implement global initiatives on sustainable development. For example, the PRME can help nurture the sustainability mindset among students and encourage them to work on local community issues.

Bibliography

2016 Policy Address. Retrieved from www.policyaddress.gov.hk/2016/eng
Achua, J.K. 2008. "Corporate Social Responsibility in Nigerian Banking System." *Society and Business Review 3*, no. 1, pp. 57–71.
Babbie, E. 2001. *The Practice of Social Research*. US: Wadsworth.
Bajunid, I.A. 2014. "The Powerhouses of Education: The Development of Scholar Teachers and Enlightened Citizenry." *The 17TH UNESCO-APEID International Conference*, Bangkok.
Beynaghi, A., G. Trencher, F. Moztarzadeh, M. Mozafari, R. Maknoon, and W.L. Filho. 2016. "Future Sustainability Scenarios for Universities: Moving Beyond the United Nations Decade of Education for Sustainable Development." *Journal of Cleaner Production 112*, pp. 3404–78.
Brewerton, P., and L. Millward. 2001. *Organizational Research Methods*. London: SAGE Publications Ltd.
Business Ethics. Retrieved from www.business-ethics.com/FourIdeasReform.htm
Cajazeira, J.E.R. 2008. *Executive Briefing of ISO 26000 Guidance on Social Responsibility and HKQAA-HSBC CSR Index*. Hong Kong: Hong Kong Quality Assurance Agency (HKQAA) Symposium.
Coetzee, P., and H. Fourie. 2009. "Perceptions on the Role of the Internal Audit Function in Respect of Risk." *African Journal of Business Management 3*, no. 13, pp. 959–68.

Colley, et al. 2005. *What is Corporate Governance?* New York: McGraw Hill.

Deep, D. 2007. *CSR in Practice.* New York: Palgrave Macmillan.

Djordjevic, A., and Cotton, D.R.E. 2011. "Communicating the Sustainability Message in Higher Education Institutions." *International Journal of Sustainability in Higher Education,* 12(4), pp. 381–94.

Drucker, P.F. 2006. *Classic Drucker.* US: Harvard Business School Publishing Corporation.

Drucker, F.P. 1999. *Management Challenges for the 21st Century.* New York: HarperCollins Publishers, Inc.

Education 2030. Incheon Declaration and Framework for Action in Portuguese. Retrieved from www.unesco.org/new/en/brasilia/about-this-office/single-view/news/education_2030_incheon_declaration_and_and_framework_for_ac

Galbraith, J.K. 1996. *The Good Society.* New York: Hougton Mifflin Company.

Government Releases Report on Manpower Projection to 2018. Retrieved from www.info.gov.hk/gia/general/201204/13/P20120413020.htm

Hang Seng Bank. Retrieved from http://bank.hangseng.com/1/2/about-us/corporate-responsibility

Ho, S.K.M. 1998. *ISO 9000 and Total Quality Management.* Hong Kong: HKBU Business School and Authors.

Ho, S.K. 1997. *Are ISO 9000 and TQM Routes for Business Excellence?* Paper presented at the Second International Conference on ISO 9000 and Total Quality Management, University of Luton, UK.

Jorge E.R.C. 2008. *Stakeholder Consensus Enables ISO 26000 on Social Responsibility to Move Up in Development Status.* Retrieved from www.iso.org/iso/pressrelease.htm?refid=Ref1158

MacDonaldd, L.M., and S. Rundle-Thiele. 2008. "Corporate Social Responsibility and Bank Customer Satisfaction." *International Journal of Bank Marketing 26,* no. 3, pp. 170–82.

McEwen, W.J. 2008. "When the Going Gets Tough." *The Gallup Management Journal.* Retrieved from http://gmj.gallup.com

Mcllroy, D.H. 2008. "Regulating Risks: A Measured Response to the Banking Crisis." *Journal of Banking Regulation 9,* no. 4, pp. 284–92.

Morrison, R. 2008. "The Financial Crisis Shows Us the Way." *New Hampshire Business Review,* pp. 7–20.

OECD work on Youth. Retrieved from www.oecd.org/youth.htm

Palazzo, G., and U. Richter. 2005. "CSR Business as Usual? The Case of the Tobacco Industry." *Journal of Business Ethics* 61, no. 4, pp. 387–401.

Richardson, B., L. Montanheiro, and B. O'cinneide. 1995. *How to Research, Write, Teach and Publish Management Case Studies*. UK: Pavic Publications, Sheffield Hallam University.

Ryan, A., and D. Tilbury. 2013. "Flexible Pedagogies: New Pedagogical Ideas." *The Higher Education Academy*. http://flexed.sfu.ca/wp-content/uploads/2014/10/npi_report.pdf (accessed on August 31, 2017).

Shani A.B.R., and P. Docherty. 2003. *Learning by Design—Building Sustainable Organziations*. US: Blackwell Publishing.

Sharda, R., D. Delen, and E. Turban. 2013. *Business Intelligence, A Managerial Perspective on Analytics*. New Jersey: Pearson.

The United Nations Economic Commission for Europe. Retrieved from www.unece.org/oes/nutshell/2004-2005/focus_sustainable_development.html

United Nations Global Compact. Retrieved from www.un.org/sustainabledevelopment/sustainable-development-goals

United Nations Global Issues. Retrieved from www.un.org/en/globalissues/environment/

Wirtenberg, J. 2009. *The Sustainable Enterprise Fieldbook*. New York: AMACOM Books.

Wheeler, D., and M. Sillanpaa. 1997. *The Stakeholder Corporation*. London: Pitman Publishing.

Yeung, S.M.C. 2006. "School Culture and ISO 9001: 2000 Requirement—A House of Quality School." *Asia International Open University 4*, no. 1.

Yeung, S.M.C. 2011. The Role of Banks in Corporate Social Responsibility. *Journal of Applied Economics and Business Research* 1, no. 2, pp. 103–15. Retrieved from www.aebrjournal.org/current-issue.html

Yeung, S.M.C. 2015. "Using ISO (PDCA) and SCOR (PSMD) Concepts for Strategic Partnership." *International Journal of Six Sigma and Competitive Advantage (IJSSCA) 9*, no. 1.

Annexure 4.1

Strategic Goals of HSMC

1. To afford a modern and stimulating campus environment (SG 1) to facilitate and support teaching and learning activities.
2. To develop and offer innovative academic programs (SG 2) that respond to changing community needs.
3. To provide a holistic and challenging educational experience for students (SG 3).
4. To cultivate students' global perspective (SG 4) through internationalization.
5. To develop strategic partnerships (SG 5) with industries and businesses.
6. To create internship opportunities (SG 6) for students to gain practical experience in the workplace.
7. To encourage and support dynamic research (SG 7) initially focusing on regional relevance and gradually broadening to more extensive horizons.
8. To strengthen governance structure (SG 8) .
9. To enhance quality control (SG 9) through internal and external monitoring.
10. To explore new ways and sources of funding (SG 10) to augment the financial base of the College.

Annexure 4.2

Table 4.1 CCSI-initiated events to promote sustainability (2015)

Purpose	Stakeholders	Activities
Generate awareness, buy in	Students, academics, industries, government, and NGOs	Organized Forum on Sustainable Development in Higher Education in partnership with UNESCO and APEID Example: • Seminar with keynote speaker from the Hong Kong government on sociocultural issues to empower women with entrepreneurship opportunities with sponsorship from industries

(Continued)

Table 4.1   *(Continued)*

Purpose	Stakeholders	Activities
		• Seminar with keynote speaker of Nobel Prize winner in chemistry on socio-environmental issues to increase awareness of chemicals with entrepreneurship opportunities with sponsorship from industries Launched executive training Example: Delivered responsible management training to terminal-related machinery business practitioners to increase awareness of responsible management with outcomes of: reengineering warehouse; information management; and responsible and ethical dealer management
Define strategy and generate concept of new products and services addressing UNSDGs and UNPRME	Students, academics, industries, and NGOs	Organized community-related activities for engaging stakeholders at different generations for accommodation and projects coproduction Example: A book written by undergraduate students of case institution with entrepreneurship stories provided by industries
Organize resources	Students, academics, industries, and NGOs	Offered free training to BBA-SCM students to enhance relevant skills for a sustainability mind-set Example: Free innovative training on Design Thinking and Visual Product Management conducted by film director and NGO
Generate intellectual capital	Students, academics, industries, government, and NGOs	Conducted research-related activities for ongoing dialogue with stakeholders Example: Submitted proposals with faculty members and other institutions to the government and NGOs for funding to support research-based activities

APEID, Asian Programme of Educational Innovation for Development.

Annexure 4.3

Outcomes of CCSI's partnerships

Research related outcomes:

Cross-disciplinary dialogues.

Conference papers on Sustainability, Six Sigma and Competitiveness.

Books on Entrepreneurship transformation and Corporate Sustainability.

Teaching/Training Outcomes:

Stories on Sustainable Development written by students for UN Flourish Prizes.

Videos shot by students on Sustainable Development, quality management, corporate social responsibility, entrepreneurship

Administrative outcomes:

Signed MoU with the UN Office for South-South Cooperation for more joint activities.

PART II

Case Studies on Course-Level Interventions to Promote Responsible Management

CHAPTER 5

Responsible Management Education: Course-Level Interventions Discussed at the Pre-Forum Workshop in the 6th PRME Asia Forum[1]

Ranjini Swamy

Goa Institute of Management

Introduction

To practice responsible management, business school students must acquire appropriate cognitive and affective competencies through the curriculum. Some competencies discussed earlier include (a) an understanding of the relationship between business, society and the natural environment; (b) an ability to diagnose and solve complex problems by drawing on multiple perspectives; (c) a compassion and empathy for underprivileged people who are treated unjustly. This chapter shares the philosophy, broadcourse outline, and pedagogy adopted by a few business school faculty members to inculcate some of these competencies. It draws from presentations and discussions during the pre-Forum Workshop, where faculty members from different business schools shared their course designs.

---

[1] Based on the proceedings of the workshop on Teaching Responsible Management held as part of the 6th PRME Asia Forum at Goa, India, in November 2015.

Responsible management is taught through stand-alone courses or in modules/sessions within discipline-based courses. Stand-alone courses include courses on Ethics and Sustainability, Business Ethics and Corporate Responsibility, Marketing and Sustainability, and Managing Sustainability. Modules in existing courses include the adoption of the Giving Voice to Values (GVV) approach in a course on Sales and Distribution, and introduction of the stakeholder approach in a course "Agricultural Entrepreneurship."

Stand-Alone Courses on Responsible Management

"Managing Sustainability" Offered at the Indian Institute of Management, Ahmedabad[2]: Courses on Responsible Management have to help students explore what is corporate responsibility, to whom a corporation is responsible and for what. Professor. Rama Mohana Turaga and Professor Vaibhav Bhamoriya address these issues in a course titled "Managing Sustainability" offered at the Indian Institute of Management, Ahmedabad (IIMA) India[3]. The premise of the course is that business is embedded in a larger network of stakeholders and has a responsibility toward their wellbeing. The course explores the responsibility of business toward its stakeholders and what can be done to better embed sustainability as a value. It explores the perspective of various "actors" (stakeholders) on issues that broadly fall within the domain of sustainability.

Prof. Turaga demonstrated the use of a case-study to generate a discussion on ethics, corporate responsibility and sustainable development. Workshop participants discussed the dilemma faced by an executive of a well-known multinational supplier of power and automation equipment. This company had contracted with a power company to supply and install equipment to help build a large dam at Laos[4] in South East Asia. The power company in turn had contracted with the government

---

[2] Based on presentation and discussion led by Prof. Rama Mohana Turaga at the 6th PRME Asia Forum, Goa, India, in 2015.

[3] IIMA is an autonomous institute set up by the Government of India and known for use of the case method of teaching.

[4] Laos was one of the poorest countries in south east Asia.

of Laos to resettle the displaced inhabitants elsewhere. When the power company did not keep its commitment of resettling the displaced inhabitants, an international NGO took up the issue and exerted pressure on the project financiers to resolve the issue. What was the responsibility of the multinational equipment supplier that was helping build the dam? Did it have any obligation to respond? Who is ultimately responsible for the displacement of large sections of people to construct a dam—the company that contracts to resettle the displaced people or all stakeholders (including the local government and the financiers) who stand to benefit from the project? More generally, what is the responsibility of the companies toward society: mere legal compliance or something more? Could something that is legal automatically qualify as ethical? For example, if it is legal to slap someone, then is it automatically moral and ethical also? What is ethical? When people who benefit from corporate action are different from and greater in number than those who lose from it, how should the company respond toward the latter? Should a utilitarian perspective be adopted or should moral arguments find space in deciding how to respond? These were some of the interesting questions that were explored.

A critical challenge in teaching the course is the lack of relevant case studies that are embedded in the Indian context. The instructors supplement the few such cases with videos and other written materials to facilitate a discussion about ethics, corporate responsibility and sustainable development in the Indian context. The instructors avoid catalogued cases of Harvard or Ivey for teaching the course as these are often embedded in a different context.

Teaching the course also posed a personal dilemma. Prof Turaga's own values made him uncomfortable with the exclusive application of the utilitarian perspective, especially when the poor were adversely affected by business action. How could he create space for a moral perspective (as against the utilitarian perspective) in the classroom discussions on responsibility? This could require that students imagine themselves in the position of the affected people and experience as closely as possible their suffering. However, not many MBA students can get into the shoes of the poor and empathize with them in such situations. Inculcating a sensitivity to the poor thus remains a challenge.

"Marketing and Sustainability" Offered at Xavier University, Bhubaneswar, India[5]: Specialized courses on Marketing, Finance, Operations and Human resources also need to explore and reinforce the concept of corporate responsibility toward its stakeholders. Thus Marketing courses need to explore the responsibility of marketers toward the company's customers, wholesalers and retailers. Professor Subhasis Ray does just that in the course "Marketing and Sustainability" offered at the Xavier University, Bhubaneswar, India, and at several foreign universities. The course examines how marketers are doing their job and what are its consequences for stakeholders.

According to Professor Ray, the traditional approach to marketing focussed on how to price, package and distribute the product and how to get maximum value from the customer. This has led to a very problematic image for marketers—they are often seen as *con guys*, who are out to take advantage of the customer. (On a lighter vein, if a product is carcinogenic, the marketing people will say the product will help customers appreciate life!) The growing discussion on sustainability called for marketers to take more responsibility for the consequences of their actions. There was need for a normative approach to marketing, where students could explore and understand how marketing is affecting society—how marketing is forcing consumerism, how it is trying to make a consumer out of little children, and how it is pushing products.

The course "Marketing and Sustainability" aims to adopt a normative approach to marketing. It is offered as an elective over 20 sessions, each of 11/2 hours. The first part of the course explores the current challenges of marketing (e.g., decreasing trust) and makes a case for sustainability and stakeholder-centric marketing orientations. In the second part, the course explores socio-ecological problems like mounting garbage and the opportunities these provide to marketers to create "shared value." Examples of companies in Asia are used to illustrate shared value creation. The message is that corporations can do good and also have a good market at the same

---

[5] Based on the presentation by Prof. Subhasis Ray, Xavier University, Bhubaneswar, India, and the discussions that followed at the pre-Forum Workshop on Teaching Responsible Management, 6th PRME Asia Forum, 2015.

time. In the third part, marketing and sustainability are discussed with a normative twist.

Students who take the course are primarily interested in job placement. It is difficult for them to stay attentive over the entire duration of the session. They do not like to read long articles. Written submissions often do not capture original thinking.

In keeping with this context, the sessions are characterized by multiple student-centric activities. The sessions start with 30 to 40 minutes of lectures/discussion of the articles or a case study. The students are then divided into groups, and asked to prepare for a debate-cum-discussion on a specific topic. Each group researches online using mobiles (each classroom has wifi), and then participates in the debate. The use of cell phones for researching the topic helps the students stay focused in the classroom. At the end of each class, the groups are expected to write down the learning from the case/article and mobile-based research in a learning journal. The learning journal promotes thinking and reflection during the class. The learning journal entries are submitted to the instructor for assessment. The instructor randomly picks any four to five submissions for grading. The course also familiarizes students with the perspectives of other stakeholders affected by marketing decisions. It requires students to interview some of the stakeholders. This exercise forces students to think at least for an hour about what to ask, how to interpret answers, what is the learning from the interview, and so on. The interview transcript—used only for academic purposes—is also a deliverable.

Prof. Ray shared some of the challenges faced in conducting the course. The first challenge is positioning the course. Students appear to prefer courses with an emphasis on marketing; they are not enthused by courses with "too much" emphasis on sustainability. So there is a need to position the course as a marketing course and not a sustainability course. The second challenge is establishing the job relevance of the course. Without this, subscriptions to the course could decline. The course gets lower priority than traditional courses like Sales and Distribution, Business-2-Business (B2B) Marketing and so on. With increasing jobs available in the area of sustainability, this could become less of an issue in the future. The third challenge is the faculty member's lack of knowledge about quantitative aspects of sustainability, for example, climate change modeling. This restricts the course to a discussion of qualitative aspects of sustainability, which affects student acceptance. The fourth challenge is the lack of availability of rigorous and locally relevant learning resources on sustainability. While some Indian business schools have developed good learning resources, the dependence on Harvard Business School and Ivey case studies continues. Students are often not able to relate to the context of these case studies. The fifth challenge is the attitude of students to ethics and sustainability. Students in India tend to have different responses to ethics and sustainability than students in Finland or Japan. It is more difficult to teach these topics in India.

Business Ethics and Corporate Responsibility offered at The School of Economics and Management at Tsinghua University,[6] *China.* Reconciling the different perspectives of stakeholders can pose ethical dilemmas to decision makers. If students are not trained to address these ethical dilemmas, they may make decisions that compromise the wellbeing of the stakeholders in the longer term. To deal with various ethical dilemmas at the workplace, students need opportunities to identify such dilemmas and find ways to resolve them. Professor June Qian offers a one-credit course "Business Ethics and Corporate Responsibility" to make students understand ethical and sustainability challenges, realize the complexity and sensitivity of these issues and work toward ensuring that business decisions are ethical, besides being financially prudent. The course offers them several frameworks that guide decision making.

Students attending the course typically have 8 to 10 years of work experience and so are aware of the realities of business. They are not sure that the faculty members understand how to run business or the challenges therein. They believe that faculty members should not advise them on what values to have.

Initially, the teachers who were assigned to teach the course did not have any formal training in the subject. They were teaching other courses like Business Law, Statistics or Communication (soft skills). Lacking a theoretical background in the subject of Ethics and Sustainability, they decided that the best way to teach the course was through case studies

---

[6] Based on the presentation of Prof June Qian at the Workshop on Teaching Responsible Management at the 6th Prme Asia Forum.

that brought the real world ethical challenges to the classroom. During the classes, instructors also encouraged the students to share the ethical dilemmas that their managers faced.

In China, there are several challenges experienced in teaching Ethics. One, there are few case studies on Ethics in the Chinese context. Two, there is a gap between knowing and doing. The students know what is right, but they don't translate it to action. Three, ethics is not integrated into other core courses of the MBA program.

Despite this, the course has received a favorable response. The university gave the course instructors a top prize on their achievement in educating students about corporate social responsibility and ethics. The instructors have shared their experiences with other academics at national conferences and seminars. They have also helped faculty members at other universities to teach courses on Ethics. They also do research on Ethics.

Ethics and Sustainability Offered at Bhutan and University of Auckland, New Zealand[7]: Dealing with ethical dilemmas requires decision makers to become sensitive to their own values and those of others. Professor Ross MacDonald addresses this issue in a course "Organizational Ethics and Sustainability" offered to undergraduate business students at New Zealand, Bhutan, and other countries. He uses students' experiences in the classroom to generate an involved discussion on ethics and sustainability. These experiences also help students develop an insight into their own values and those of others.

In his view, typical courses on ethics and sustainability give lot of intellectual information to students. They tend to be prescriptive and promote ethical behavior through guilt. However, ethics education should be about opening minds. It should leave students with more questions than answers, more confusion (constructive) than certainty. The message should be that ethics and sustainability are positive things—ethical behavior should not be guilt-induced.

A challenge instructors face in teaching ethics and sustainability is addressing the gap between the world of business and the world of

---

[7] Based on the lecture-cum-demonstration of Prof. Ross MacDonald, University of Auckland, in the pre-Forum Workshop on Teaching Responsible Management at the 6th PRME Asia Forum, Goa, India, in 2015.

ethics/sustainability. People who see business as a process that should create profits find it difficult to comprehend the language/arguments of those concerned about ethics and vice versa. So what could be done to reduce the gap between these two distinct perspectives? The link between the two perspectives is the values that are held, shared and negotiated by people. When students work in organizations later, they are going to work with their thinking, their values and their intuition in that context, at that moment. So if the students can work with their values in a classroom, they ought to.

To identify the core or ultimate values, there is a need to ask more fundamental questions. In Bhutan, which subscribes to the philosophy of gross national happiness, people ask a fundamental question that so many business schools don't—"what is business and the economy for?" Business has become an end in itself whereas it ought to be helping us to become fully human. That is its purpose. Without that, business is losing its moral purpose and its ethical legitimacy.

Professor MacDonald described in detail, how he got students to explore their ultimate values and those of others in the classroom. He starts by asking undergraduates a very simple question: *Do you think that the world in 15 years of time is going to be better or worse?* Students discuss the question in groups of four and reach a consensus in 20 minutes. In his experience, more young people believe that the world is likely to be in a worse condition. However, the decision is not as important as the animated discussion it generates. While evaluating whether the world will be better or worse, students are implicitly working with values.

Next, students discuss "What did you think would be better or worse?" This is where the learning starts. What do they mean when they say the world will be a better or a worse place? What criteria are they using? There are long and vigorous discussions in the groups as members attempt to find consensus on the criteria. They share feelings, argue, and gradually shape their vague ideas into quite solid concepts. In the process they implicitly explore values. Students tend to say they want a sustainable, inclusive, peaceful, and healthful world. They want a world that is not depleted of its resources, is efficient in resource use, and has plenty for other species too. They want a world that is more inclusive, less polarized/unequal and with less incidence of extreme poverty. They want a world of fulfillment or happiness or well-being. So there is a similar constellation of values emerging across many students that represents their vision of the future.

Once the constellation of values that define a better world are established, the class explores how to make their vision a reality in the subsequent 15 years.[8] The instructor asks them: "What would they do, as business students, to create the world they want to live in?" They discuss what they are willing to do to achieve a better world and what they would be willing to give up to have a more equal world. They explore whether they would give up international travel, the food they presently eat, the clothing they wear, the car that they want to but may not be allowed to drive. And so the question begins to deepen and they battle these things out in small groups until they have a robust agreement. It becomes clear to the students that if they are just going to sit back and expect somebody else to realize their vision, that would not work. So now the students discuss how they are going to be part of a constructive process of change.

Professor MacDonald then challenges the students to think about the human characteristics that would be needed to make that vision a reality. An example of a human characteristic is forgiveness. Over the next 15 minutes, the students discuss in groups and come to a consensus on five critical human capacities required to realize their vision.[9] To arrive at a consensus students must learn to stand up for their values. The instructor "cruises around" and asks groups whether there are any questions before they actually start the process.

After the discussion, students are encouraged to move to another group, discuss and reach a consensus on another set of human characteristics. This process can generate an amazing diversity of ideas. Moreover, the presence of small safe discussion environments allows students to jointly explore these ideas, build their own conclusions, and reach a consensus. In the process, they explore the roots of their thinking, explore

---

[8] It is important because we often think in a short cycle. To think 15 years ahead is constructive because it is long enough as things can change and short enough to be tangible. So this becomes a possibility of empowerment.

[9] Everybody in the group has to talk, everybody gets to express his or her opinion. If somebody is talking too much, it is the group's responsibility to put him or her in line.

differences and/or similarities among concepts (e.g., intolerance and racism), and discover commonalities. This part can be empowering.

Students come up with the human characteristics necessary for building a better future that is more sustainable, more inclusive, and more harmonious. They talk of the need to be courageous, creative, and persevering. These are all important values. Professor MacDonald then points out that any terrorist who enters a territory and shoots people needs these characteristics. Creativity can help create evil. So what "ultimate" values are essential for attaining the kind of world students want? The students go back to discussing this in small groups to generate a modified list of four to five ultimate values. Some ultimate values that get shared after this discussion are: (a) compassion; (b) generosity, the ability to give yourself to others; and (c) self-restraint, the ability to control one's emotions and actions.

As students explore visions and actions over a 15-year span, they are forced to think long term. As they argue about the important human characteristics, they bring their ultimate values into the conscious, thereby deepening themselves. They realize that these values are not absolute or shared; they need to be negotiated and modified to achieve a consensus. Students engage in a process of self-verification and they find it fantastic because it is deep within them.

The instructor plays a facilitating role during this process. First, he or she needs to directly interact with the students. Unfortunately, in many classrooms, PowerPoint presentations have become an intermediary force, with students looking at the PowerPoint and the instructor talking to the PowerPoint—there is no real interaction between students and teacher. Second, the instructor has to decide how much to intervene in the discussion, and whether to share his or her values with the students. The instructor could personally have great difficulty accepting situations where a vast majority of people have suffering in their lives. However, in sharing his or her values with the students, the instructor runs the risk of students dismissing this input—their gazes could "become more distant." So the instructor needs to work with the students' values as much as possible and make them explicit. Student engagement is more likely when their values become the bedrock of the educational process.

Students are often aware that there could be challenges in translating values into action at the workplace. They wonder whether values like generosity or compassion are practical in a competitive world. Professor MacDonald responds to this with a counter question "How many of you think generosity to be unimportant?" If some students concur, he asks them to take out their cell phones and text their mother or a close friend that generosity is not practical. For the students, making such a statement to their near and dear could be challenging. This needs to be complemented by a strong message that practicing the ultimate values such as compassion or generosity need not require "walking against the facts and figures of the company."

Modules on Responsible Management in Existing Courses

Module on Stakeholder identification and management in "Agricultural Entrepreneurship" at the Indian Institute of Management, Ahmedabad (IIMA):

Sometimes, the stakeholders of business are not visible and yet could be strongly affected by business decisions. Professor Vaibhav Bhamoriya helps students identify such stakeholders and address their concerns through an elective course on Agricultural Entrepreneurship in the Agri-Business Management Programme at IIMA, India. The course aims to "corrupt" students of the program into becoming entrepreneurs! It also aims to make students conscious of the stakeholders who are not visible and are yet impacted by actions of the entrepreneurs. It helps students examine the impact of entrepreneurial decisions on the wellbeing of such stakeholders.

Videos and supplementary articles are used to present a case study and explore issues pertaining to stakeholder management. In Professor Bhamoriya's view, the use of case studies exposes students to the practical challenges of entrepreneurship. However, using case studies as a method of instruction is not easy for the following reasons: It is a user-centered method of learning, where the outcome is a function of what the users (in this case, learners) want to do with it. Again, in his experience, most case studies do not really include the perspectives of all stakeholders.

Professor Bhamoriya demonstrated how he used videos and supplementary materials to identify "invisible" stakeholders of a farmer-entrepreneur and help address their concerns. The video presented the water scarcity facing almond farmers in California, the economic impact of this scarcity on the farmer-entrepreneurs, their responses and the reactions of some stakeholders to these responses. Conventionally, any entrepreneur would analyze the impact of water scarcity on his or her profits alone and use this analysis to decide whether to stay or leave the business. Students follow a similar pattern. However, Professor Bhamoriya helps students to see the impact of the farmer-entrepreneur's decision on several stakeholders who are not visible. A large agricultural producer who decides to leave the business due to water scarcity could adversely impact consumers and investors' sentiments. Less obvious is the impact on commodity markets and on other small producers, on producers of other crops in the area. Students who initially did not pay attention to these stakeholders begin to see that an entrepreneur's decision does not exist in a vacuum. They learn map the stakeholders, examine the impact of each action-alternative on their interests and arrive at solutions to address their wellbeing and that of the farmer-entrepreneur.

Students see the need for new business models to sustain the growers, the processors, and other stakeholders while protecting the interests of the farmer-entrepreneur. They realize that more collaboration, going back and forth between stakeholders, is needed to find a solution that works for all. While this looks very simple, it is very difficult to operationalize.

The GVV approach applied in B2B Marketing and Sales and Distribution Courses Offered at Xavier University, Bhubaneswar, India[10]: To practice responsible management, students need to identify the values shared by different stakeholders and learn how to implement these values at the workplace. Effective implementation of some values—such as compassion, justice, anti-corruption—at the workplace may not be easy. There are many situations where decision makers know what is the right thing to do in the circumstances but don't know how to effectively implement

---

[10] Based on the presentations by Prof. Mary Gentile and Prof. Subhasis Ray and the discussion that followed at the pre-Forum workshop on Teaching Responsible Management at the 6th PRME Asia Forum, Goa, India, in 2015.

them at the workplace. To reduce this knowing-doing gap, Professor Sub-hasis Ray has included a module on Giving Voice to Values (GVV) in his Marketing Electives (B2B Marketing and Sales and Distribution).

The GVV approach was pioneered by Prof. Mary Gentile as a new and innovative approach to values-driven leadership development. The approach was developed with support from the Aspen Institute and Yale School of Management. The GVV approach has been integrated into business school curricula across the world, including in some business schools in India and China.

The GVV approach emerged as a response to Prof. Gentile's own frustrations with the way ethics was taught in the business schools in the late 1990s. Typically, students of an Ethics course were given a deci-sion-making situation and asked, "what is the right thing to do in this particular business situation?" Students became aware of ethical dilemmas and learnt to apply different moral reasoning perspectives to analyze the decision situations. They discovered that being ethical was difficult and not practical. They emerged from ethics classes feeling disempowered. The result was that a study of ethics did not guide action.

A new approach to teaching ethics was needed. Research about habit formation, behavior of people in groups, and brain plasticity suggested that there could be other more effective approaches to teaching ethics. Ideas also came from kinesiology, the study of physical movement. Prof. Gentile observed that during classes on self-defense, trainees were taught the physical movements and then practiced their moves against a man in a parade suit who attacked them with full force when it was least expected. This forced the trainees to be in a state of preparedness to defend themselves. The approach was based on a concept called "specific state muscle memory": If trainees rehearsed something in the physio-logical, intellectual, and emotional state that closely paralleled reality, then even if they froze, their body remembered what was rehearsed and enacted it. In other words, rehearsal of skills created a muscle memory, a default behavior. She wondered whether a moral muscle memory could be built on a similar principle. What if rehearsal was important to cre-ate such a moral muscle memory? This formed the basis of the GVV approach.

The GVV approach, in a nutshell, assumes that in many decision situations, decision-makers are clear about what is the right thing to do. The GVV approach asks, "knowing what is right, how could you get it done effectively?" Using GVV case studies, students are encouraged to temporarily assume they want to do the right thing. They work in groups to develop an action plan and "scripts" to effectively implement the right thing. The action plan and scripts are presented to peers for improving their effectiveness. The continued rehearsal across several practical situations creates a "specific state muscle memory," or a default behavior that is more likely to be translated into workplace behavior.

The GVV approach enables students who are "idealists"[11] and "pragmatists"[12] to acquire the skills, the confidence, and the default behavior to do the right thing and live by their values at the workplace. GVV cases describe how managers successfully dealt with ethical dilemmas at the workplaces.[13] When "opportunists"[14] see the benefits of enacting the right thing at the workplace, some of them could begin to do the same.

The approach got early support from business schools in India. Prof. Subhasis Ray was one of the early adopters. He experienced value conflicts in his experience as an executive in sales and marketing. Later, while teaching marketing, many asked him how to deal with value conflicts, say when there is a demand for bribe. In his view, the GVV approach offers a way of helping students address value conflicts in sales and marketing situations. Some benefits: First, it is practical and provides access to real-life case studies of executives who successfully defended their values. Second, the analogy of a "moral muscle" appeals. Repeated rehearsal of

---

[11] According to Prof. Mary Gentile, Idealists are students who prefer to act on their values even if it puts them at a disadvantage.

[12] According to Prof. Mary Gentile, Pragmatists are students who would like to act on their values as long as it does not put them at its systematic disadvantage.

[13] Some GVV cases illustrate situations where the manager was not able to act on his values. The instructor could use the case to ask why his or her strategy did not work and what would the students do in the situation to be more successful. Students become consultants and coaches in the situation.

[14] According to Prof. Mary Gentile, Opportunists are people who prefer to do whatever it takes to maximize their material self-interest.

doing the right thing could increase the chance that a manager could keep his or her values intact without becoming a martyr and losing his or her job.

Prof. Ray exposes students to case studies describing typical situations faced by marketers, including value conflicts. For instance, regulatory authorities in a new market may demand a bribe for permitting the company to market its products. The decision-maker may be personally against giving such bribes. How could he meet business goals without bribing people? The decision-maker needs to develop an action plan that addresses the following issues: Who are the stakeholders and how is each affected by the decision to bribe/not bribe the authorities? What reasons and rationalizations would he encounter in support of bribing? (Typical arguments include "everyone does it" and "you can't survive in business or reach your targets without bribing.") How could he counter these arguments? Who is likely to support his stand? Where is the opportunity to establish a common purpose with the stakeholders? How can he obtain the cooperation from them for his plans? Once such an action plan is made, it is presented to peers and rehearsed in class. Peers provide coaching to improve the effectiveness of the action plan and script. This entire process can take two to three hours. To develop the moral muscle, students need an opportunity to practice the GVV approach over six to eight cases.

While discussing the case, Prof. Ray prefers to distance himself from the value conflicts in the case study, as GVV just enables people to practice *their* values. He prefers not to preach or impose his values. The student finally has to decide whether he or she is going to use those skills as a marketer and as a manager.

The GVV approach illustrates that as marketers, it is possible to do the right thing and still achieve business goals. Although it is not easy to live by one's values at the workplace and it is not even always possible, it is important. And one can get better at it. Students learn to balance the short-term and the long-term goals. They see that succumbing to the short-term pressures could become an addictive cycle that compounds problems and compromises the longer-term business purpose. As future executives, they need to see themselves as agents of continuous improvement, not as whistle-blowers.

Summary

To act responsibly as managers, students need to learn various cognitive and affective competencies. They need to understand the concept of responsibility, why organizations need to behave responsibly toward their stakeholders and how to enact responsible behavior. Inculcating these competencies is challenging, given the profile of MBA students in Asia. Students appear to be aware of the social and environmental challenges facing society. They desire a more sustainable, inclusive, healthful, and peaceful society. However, they are yet to see why business should be involved in creating a sustainable society and are skeptical about the practicality of this idea. As potential managers seeking jobs, they are focused on the job relevance of courses. They believe that their job prospects are improved if they develop functional knowledge and skills. They are not sure how courses or modules on ethics and sustainability will help them get jobs.

The chapter details how various faculty members address these challenges in stand-alone courses or in modules on responsible management. They tend to build on the concerns of students, allow them to learn from each other through multiple activities within and outside the classroom, and provide them with opportunities to practice application and reflect on this experience. These pedagogies help enhance the cognitive understanding of the concept of responsibility and provide opportunities to develop the skills needed to implement responsible management. However, generating empathy and compassion for stakeholders who are not visible or who are poor remains challenging.

CHAPTER 6

Course on Marketing Ethics at the Indian Institute of Management, Indore: A Reflection

Jayasankar Ramanathan and Biswanath Swain

Indian Institute of Management Indore, India

Background

The consumers in India have become sensitive to the techniques that the marketers use in promoting their products. Before buying any goods or services, they have started examining whether the given goods or services are worthy of buying or not. Various consumer organizations have come up to assist consumers in their fight against unethical actions of the marketers.[1] They have educated consumers through various consumer-empowering seminars and discussions. Being more aware, consumers have made the marketers redress their faulty goods and services.[2] The Government of India has also constituted the Department of Consumers Affairs (DCA)[3] under its Ministry of Consumer Affairs, Food and Public Distribution, to protect the interests of the consumer

---

[1] See http://consumersindia.org and http://www.cehat.org/go/BnhraWeb/Consumer (accessed on June 16, 2016).

[2] http://consumer.org.in/?q=page/achievements (accessed on June 21, 2016).

[3] http://consumeraffairs.nic.in/home.aspx (accessed on June 16, 2016).

through various effective legislations (e.g., The Consumer Protection Act, 1986; The Consumer Protection Rules, 1987; and Consumer Protection Regulation, 2005).[4] Thus, if an organization that markets products (marketer) is found involved in any form of unethical practice or corporate abuse, the affected consumer(s) with the help of these government or nongovernmental organizations could challenge the marketer in the court. As a result, the marketer may end up paying crores of rupees as fine, besides experiencing a decrease in sales gain and market share.

Consumer action against errant marketers is facilitated by the presence of social media. An airline company's unprofessional behavior toward a passenger and his tweet[5] is a case in point. The passenger's luggage was tagged to a wrong destination. His family members' waitlisted tickets were not confirmed despite seats being available. He witnessed poor customer service by the staff of the airline company. Upon reacting to the service provided to him, the passenger tweeted that he is "Angry Disappointed and Frustrated" with the "don't care attitude" of the staffs of the airline company.[6] Following this tweet, many of his followers started jeopardizing the airline company with negative comments on the Twitter. Due to the unfavorable comments about the airline company in Twitter and the resultant furor, the airline company apologized for the mistake,[7] dealt the issue in a very conscientious way, and finally resolved the same. Given the power of the social media, the concerned airline company could have responded more professionally before its brand image was adversely impacted.

Marketers of socially controversial products like tobacco and alcohol and environmentally incompatible products like plastic bags, plastic

---

[4] http://consumeraffairs.nic.in/forms/contentpage.aspx?lid=640 (accessed on June 16, 2016).

[5] http://dailymail.co.uk/indiahome/indianews/article-3317610/British-Airways-mocked-20-000-cricket-fans-losing-Sachin-Tendulkar-s-luggage.html (accessed on June 16, 2016).

[6] http://mirror.co.uk/sport/cricket/sachin-tendulkar-gets-british-airways-6824005 (accessed on January 19, 2017).

[7] http://indianexpress.com/article/sports/cricket/sachin-tendulkar-gets-angry-at-british-airways-for-dont-care-attitude/ (accessed on January 19, 2017).

water bottles, disposable cutlery, single-use disposable razors, food pack-aging items, and so on, are harmful not only for the concerned consum-ers, but also for all others who are co-inhabiting with them. For example, the tobacco products are not only detrimental to the targeted consum-ers, but also for the coworkers, family members, and waiters. A study of tobacco consumption and its effects suggests that one million tobacco deaths happen every year in India and one person dies every six seconds due to tobacco use.[8] In addition, India has been considered as the country that has the highest number of smokeless tobacco deaths.[9] Similarly, the environmentally incompatible products, stored as waste or garbage, emit toxic elements to the environment, which not only affect the people in the concerned locality, but also the ecology. Marketers of such products usually claim that they are neither advertising about such products nor persuading the people to buy. Yet, one could argue that they are tacitly targeting consumers who are addicted and the consumers who are vulner-able to such addictive products.

There is a widespread perception in the common parlance that in order for a marketer to become successful in his or her business, she has to be unethical. This is partly attributable to the lack of awareness about legal[10] and other developments in the Indian context, along with the absence of rational foresight and we-feeling within the marketers. Par-ticipants of business schools, including those who are at the early stage of their professional careers, are unlikely to be abreast of the nuances of Asian/Indian context in which marketing of goods or services takes place. Hence, there is a need of a course like Marketing Ethics to sensitize them toward ethical marketing.

---

[8] http://hindustantimes.com/india/one-million-tobacco-deaths-in-india-every-year-yet-politicians-in-denial/story-AlCLK66RW6xi9raARYVXdL.html (accessed on November 10, 2016).

[9] http://dnaindia.com/health/report-india-has-highest-number-of-smokeless-tobacco-deaths-finds-new-study-2117193 (accessed on November 10, 2016).

[10] Law is considered as moral minimum. The marketers are expected to conform, at least, to the laws.

Institution

Indian Institute of Management (IIM) Indore was established in 1996 by Department of Higher Education, Ministry of Human Resources Development, Government of India, with an objective to impart high-quality management education and training. Since its inception, IIM Indore has been acting as a leader in the field of management education, interfacing with industry, government sector, and public sector organizations. The mission of IIM Indore is to be a contextually relevant business school with world-class academic standards that develops socially conscious managers, leaders, and entrepreneurs. IIM Indore is committed to: (a) excellence in management education, research, and training; (b) use of contemporary participant-centric pedagogies and teaching methods; and (c) a presence in emerging segments of management education.

The participants of the Integrated Programme in Management (IPM) and Post-graduate Programme (PGP) enter the institute through different selection procedures. The duration of IPM is five years while that of PGP is two years. Participants of the PGP join the institute after completing their undergraduate education in arts, commerce, science, engineering, and other such streams. Many PGP participants have few years of work experience. Participants of the IPM enter the institute after successfully completing the higher secondary education.[11] While the curriculum of the first three years of the IPM is distinct, the participants undergo the same courses as the PGP participants, in the last two years of their program. The course on marketing ethics was offered as an elective for the participants of IPM in their fifth year and for the participants of PGP in their second year.

Apart from these two programs, the institute also offers Executive Post Graduate Programme, Fellow Programme in Management (FPM), and other short-term programs. One of the goals of education at IIM Indore is to prepare business leaders with a sound understanding of ethics. Hence, IIM Indore offers core courses such as "Ethics and CSR" for the PGP participants and "Ethics and Society" and "Contemporary

[11] http://iimidr.ac.in/academic-programmes/five-year-integrated-programme-in-management-ipm/ (accessed October 3, 2016).

Moral Issues" for the IPM participants. To fulfill its mission, IIM Indore enhances participants' skills through workshops on "Communication," "Leadership," "Entrepreneurial Orientation," and "Innovation and Design Thinking and Sustainability." Apart from offering various other courses, the institute encourages its participants to participate in a wide range of extra- and cocurricular activities, which include IRIS (an annual management and cultural festival),[12] Utsaha (a rural marketing fest),[13] Rural Immersion Programme,[14] Himalayan Outbound Programme,[15] Industrial Visit Programme,[16] Management Canvas,[17] Voyage Club,[18] and many such activities.

The institute also encourages its participants to be involved in various programmes/activities where the participants can plan and execute initiatives to promote responsibility toward various stakeholders of the society.

One initiative is the Social Sensitivity programme. Under the programme, the participants visit various remote areas in and around Indore,[19] discuss with the denizens of these areas, and make them

---

[12] It is an annual management and cultural fest, which brings forth a fresh amalgamation of management and culture in an exhilarating three-day extravaganza.

[13] Under this program, the participants organize various workshops to make the villagers and the people living in remote areas of Indore sensitive toward their health and environment.

[14] The objective of this endeavor is to sensitize the budding managers and entrepreneurs of the Institute toward the various schemes undertaken by the government in villages and to study and analyze their execution and effectiveness.

[15] The participants go through multiple rounds of training, focusing on adventure sports and real-life challenges, designed to test their managerial and leadership skills. From rock-climbing, rappelling, and river rafting, to yoga and pranayam, the Himalayan Outbound Programme offers a mix of physical and psychological experiential tasks for the participants.

[16] The program helps keep participants abreast with the current management practices followed by such organizations and acquire traits that the industry demands of them.

[17] It is a student publication, which aspires to bring forth the ideas and models that hold the potential to change the business landscape in future.

[18] This initiative tries to bridge the gap between theory and practice of finance by conducting knowledge-sharing sessions and events. Members of the club research on various sectors, which is then shared with investors in the form of sessions, reports, and meetings.

[19] The city of Madhya Pradesh, India, where the institute is located.

aware of various issues pertaining to their health, education, and environment and the viable solutions for these issues. In addition, in their spare time, the participants visit these areas, distribute books and other study materials to the kids, and teach the kids. The objective of this program mentored by the institute is to inculcate a sense of moral responsibility in its participants toward their society and environment.

Another initiative is the Industry Interface course. Participants visit various companies in the city; sometimes, the companies share the managerial problems faced in HR, Finance and so on and seek recommendations. Participants study the company comprehensively and discuss possible solutions to resolve their problem. The objective of the course is not only to get the participants exposed to the current business dilemmas, but also to guide the participants to help the companies resolve some of the pressing problems from a holistic perspective.

Another initiative is the School adoption programme called Pragat-I or Pragati. The institute adopts some nearby schools which are attended by children from poor families. Books, pencils, sweaters and other such useful items are distributed to the school-children through the participants. In addition, the participants join the institute's staff members to teach the schoolchildren. Thus, time and again, the institute puts its best effort to inculcate a holistic management education to its participants, *en route* to make them socially responsible leaders, entrepreneurs, and managers. The course on marketing ethics is a step in that direction.

Intervention

The course "Marketing Ethics" was offered as an elective of two credits[20] to participants of the second-year PGP and participants of the fifth-year IPM. A total of 49 participants registered in the course on Marketing Ethics. Out of 49, 12 participants were from IPM and 37 participants were from PGP. Apart from that, out of 49 participants, 43 percent were

---

[20] Ten classroom contact sessions with each session being 75 minutes.

female and 57 percent were male. The authors of this chapter co-taught the course, with the assistance of two academic associates.

The course strove to make the participants aware of various ethical and unethical courses of action in the field of marketing and consider the corresponding consequences of those actions. The authors tried to motivate the participants to become ethically responsible leaders. Since the participants registered in the course were at the beginning of their professional careers, they were guided through comprehensive ethical analysis of each course of action in the field of marketing. This helped the participants develop capability to identify unethical issues in the field of marketing, differentiate the ethical courses of action from the unethical ones, and appreciate the effect of ethical/unethical courses of action. This endeavor fit well with Principles for Responsible Management Education (PRME) Principle 1 (Purpose),[21] which states that "[w]e will develop capabilities of students to be future generators of sustainable value for business and society at large and to work for an inclusive and sustainable global economy."

The course dealt with ethical/unethical business practices that usually prevail in marketing the goods or services. The topics were aligned with those discussed in basic marketing courses such as STP (Segmentation, Targeting, and Positioning), 4Ps (Product, Price, Promotion, and Place), Marketing Research, and International Marketing. The course outline with session-wise topics and readings is furnished in Annexure 6.1.

There were 10 sessions of classroom interaction with the participants, followed by a guest lecture on Consumer Protection Act. The two authors coordinated between them to deliver each session. Each session was cotaught by both the authors such that the author from the marketing area handled case discussion for almost half the duration of the session and the author from the humanities and social sciences area delivered lecture for the remaining duration of the session.

The session plan was discussed by the authors and finalized before each session. Academic associates were involved in identifying relevant video documents for each session (which were shared with participants

---

[21] http://unprme.org/about-prme/the-six-principles.php (accessed on June 13, 2016).

before, during, or after the class as appropriate) and in recording the class-room discussion of the participants.

The course was delivered using a mix of case and lecture. The authors used the video on Moral Imagination and videos on other concepts that are available in the online repository of Ethics Unwrapped (EU).[22] To make the course interesting and to make each session lively, the authors discussed relevant business cases in each session. Case discussions included various activities, such as (a) identification of unethical issue(s); (b) identification of the consequences that the concerned marketer and his or her business faced; (c) analysis and assessment of the identified unethical issue(s) in the light of the ethical principles (like golden rule,[23] silver rule,[24] and various other ethical principles pertaining to rights[25]) and some key ethical perspectives (Consequentialism, Utilitarianism, and Deontology); (d) discussion on various possible courses of action that the concerned marketer could have deliberated or might not have thought about; (e) identification of the best course of action out of possible ones; (f) discussion on implementation of the best course of action; and (g) discussion of sensitive ethical guidelines aligned with the best course of action. Lectures included presentation of different ethical issues not covered in the case, followed by discussion of ethical guidelines to resolve them.

For each case that was discussed, the authors screened video documents pertaining to the given issue. Toward the end of each session, the participants were asked to come up with viable ethical solution to the issue. The focus on the issue of implementation was aligned with the idea behind the development of Giving Voice to Values (GVV)[26] approach to teaching Ethics. The pedagogy adopted for the course fit with PRME Principle 3 (Method),[27] which states that "[w]e will create educational frameworks, materials, process and environments that enable effective learning experiences for responsible leadership."

---

[22] http://ethicsunwrapped.utexas.edu/ (accessed on June 22, 2016).

[23] Golden rule: Do unto others what you would have done unto you.

[24] Silver rule: Do not harm anyone knowingly.

[25] Rights: Right to Life, Right to Privacy, Right to Property, and Right to Choice.

[26] http://babson.edu/Academics/teaching-research/gvv/Pages/home.aspx (accessed on June 22, 2016).

[27] Ibid. (accessed on June 13, 2016).

Challenges and Outcomes

Challenges

Attracting Experts to Address Specific Cross-Disciplinary Issues

Before the beginning of the course, both the authors were with the plan to invite a judge from the District Consumer Court, Indore, to deliver a lecture either on one of the topics mentioned in the course outline or to share her experience with the participants about the verdict(s) that went in favor of consumer(s). The plan of inviting a judge to deliver a talk on a consumer court issue remained unfulfilled. The authors invited an adjunct faculty member of one of the sister IIMs, to deliver a talk on Consumer Protection Act to the participants registered in the course on marketing ethics.

Accessing Relevant Text Books/Case Studies

Since the price of the recommended (international) text books was high, it was not feasible for the library to procure as many copies of the text book as the number of the participants registered in the course. However, the library procured five copies of each book for the participants to prepare for their examination and reserved them in the reference section. During the end-term examination of the course, the participants, however, complained about the scarcity of sufficient number of copies of the recommended textbooks. A good textbook on marketing ethics rooted in the Indian/ Asian context needs to be published. Some of the participants shared their thoughts that the course could have dealt with more Indian cases, instead of using the foreign cases. Lack of good Indian cases is an area about which the authors would like to see some positive change in the future.

Ensuring Learning in Projects

To enhance the awareness of unethical practices adopted by marketers, the authors included a group project for evaluation. The project reports were to be submitted at the end of the course and were to document the unethical marketing practices at different companies located in India. To develop the project report in a systematic way, the participants were asked to follow certain guidelines. Participants were also informed that if their project report was of good quality, the concerned group would be awarded with a letter of appreciation from the authors. Even after a lot of persuasion from the authors, some of the project reports were found to be having instances of plagiarism and others did not meet the set quality standards. Those who submitted plagiarized reports were warned and informed that if they wanted to avoid "Fail" grade in the component of project report submission, they had to resubmit the report duly citing all the references. The concerned groups resubmitted the edited reports to the authors for evaluation. The authors still wonder as to how the quality of project reports from the participants can be improved in the future.

Improving Class Preparation and Participation

It was found that, at times, participants were not prepared to participate or contribute in the discussion on a given case. As a result, the discussions were not comprehensive. To make the participants read the case before the session remains a challenge.

Dealing with Scepticism

When the course on marketing ethics was underway, some of the colleagues of the authors quipped that marketing ethics is an oxymoron. Some asked the questions: "Is marketing ethics possible? Is ethics in marketing existing?" Further, one of the colleagues said that "these two people [the authors] are marketing the ethics." These light-hearted comments helped the authors appreciate some of the popular and negative views and encouraged them to build arguments for responsible management, which can lead businesses to be both ethical and successful.

Outcomes

Although the objective of the course was to make the participants realize the unethical issues involved in the field of marketing, the authors also got exposed to various new articles pertaining to the unethical issues involved in STP, 4Ps, Marketing Research, and International Marketing. The act of going through literature and analyzing issues broadened the sphere of their knowledge in the field of marketing ethics. That, further, helped the authors develop a seminar course on marketing ethics for their FPM (PhD) students. In addition, offering the course on marketing ethics gave a grand opportunity to both the authors who are from different areas of management to learn something beyond their respective areas.

Program participants who had not opted for the course on Marketing Ethics requested the authors to offer the course again in the next term. They had heard appreciative comments from the course participants about the content and delivery of the Marketing Ethics course. Since the authors were occupied with their other academic commitments and pursuits, they were however unable to offer the course in the forthcoming term. Even some of the participants registered in the course were sharing with the authors that if marketers at the beginning of their professional careers get exposed to the practices covered in the course, they may be able to think differently and will be able to deal with the business dilemmas in ethical ways.

As shared earlier, some participants were, at times, not prepared for the class discussion on a given case. In order to ensure that the participants go through the case and get prepared beforehand for the discussion in the class, the authors are planning to keep one of the components of evaluation as "one page note" (depicting the issues that the case has dealt with and some viable solutions to them) from all the students in the future editions of the course. In addition to that, the authors are planning to ask the participants to write "reflection note"—as another component of evaluation—stating the takeaway from the discussion done in the class and to submit the same at the end of every session. The objective of this component of evaluation is to make the participants comprehend and appreciate the discussion done in the class. Furthermore, that can help them value the stance that ethical course of action and profit (not unethical course of action and profit) does have the potential to bring sustainable business to marketers.

Annexure 6.1

Course Outline: Marketing Ethics

Credits: 2   Course: Elective Course   No. of Section, if elective course: 1

Instructors	E-mail:	Tel. No.	Faculty Block

Course Description

Marketing products to buyers profitably is a broad objective of each and every business organization. However, due to the fierce competition among the business organizations in the marketplace, these organizations may be tempted to take a different path to have a control over the marketplace as well as the buyers. The different path, here, refers to deceptive advertising, unfair pricing, misleading labeling, abuses of power in distribution, and so on. Such marketing practices by business organizations are usually considered questionable in terms of their ethical quotient. These practices may bring the organizations success in terms of amassing money and growth in a short term. But on the other hand, it may hamper the progress of customer retention policy and brand image of these organizations in the long run. These questionable practices may not only put the concerned business organizations in grave problem, but also destabilize the growth of society in general. And when it is found that even after some form of warning or other there is no change in their behavior, the legal domain, time and again, comes in a big way to bring them onto the track with strong and heavy penalties. An endeavor has been made in this course to make the participants aware of the ethical issues pertaining to the field of marketing.

Course Objectives

The objective of this course is to sensitize the participants toward ethical issues with respect to STP, 4Ps, marketing research, and international marketing, and orient the participants toward how one can make marketing decisions without being called unethical.

Pedagogy/Teaching Method

The pedagogy, in this course, is predominantly based on case discussions. Further if required, guest lecture(s) may be arranged depending on the availability of resource person(s). The course includes a group-based assignment in which the participants are required to identify an incident (pertaining to marketing) reported in press or in court judgment, and analyze the same in the light of one or more topics covered in this course. The assignment is expected to be rooted in the Indian context. Participants are required to execute the assignment in two phases, with phase one being proposal discussion and phase two being final report submission. Further details of this assignment will be communicated to the participants separately.

Evaluation	Weightage
Class Participation	20%
Group Based Assignment	40%
End Term	40%
Total	100%

Schedule of Sessions

Module I: Introduction to Marketing Ethics

Module Objective

The objective of this module is to introduce the participants with basic frameworks in Marketing Ethics.

Session 1: An Introduction to Marketing Ethics

Objective: To expose the participants with decision-making situations in Marketing where one may appreciate various ethical dilemmas.

Readings: Stealth Marketing: How to Reach Consumers Surreptitiously by A. M. Kaikati, J. G. Kaikati, 2004, *California Management Review*: Volume 46, Issue 4, pp. 6–22.

Case: To be distributed in the class.[28]

Session 2: Ethics and the Art of Persuasion: Developing Arguments and Positions

Objective: To make the participants aware of the ethical positions and make them develop persuasive arguments to resolve dilemmas.

Readings:

- Chapter VI: Relative, Subjective and Naturalistic Theories of Moral Standard, An Introduction to Ethics by William Lillie, Allied Publishers, 1967
- Chapter 2: Egoistic and Deontological Theories, *Ethics* by W. K. Frankena, Prentice-Hall of India, 1999, 2e
- Chapter 3: Utilitarianism, Justice and Love, *Ethics* by W. K. Frankena, Prentice-Hall of India, 1999, 2e

Case: NIL

Module II: Ethical Issues with Respect to STP and 4Ps

Module Objective

The objective of this module is to expose the participants toward the ethical issues with respect to STP and 4Ps.

Session 3: STP: Ethical Issues

Objective: To expose the participants to ethical issues in segmentation, targeting, and positioning.

Readings: Chapter 2: Ethics in researching and segmenting markets, *Ethical Marketing* by P. E. Murphy, G. R. Laczniak, N. R. Bowie, T. A. Klein, Pearson, 2004, 1e.

Case: Abercrombie and Fitch: Is it unethical to be exclusive?, 2014, Ivey, W14096.

Session 4: Product: Ethical Issues

Objective: To expose the participants to ethical issues in product management.

Readings: Chapter 3: Product management ethics, *Ethical Marketing* by P. E. Murphy, G. R. Laczniak, N. R. Bowie, T. A. Klein, Pearson, 2004, 1e.

---

[28] In session 1, the caselets distributed was prepared from Martin, K.D., and N.C. Smith. 2008. "Commercializing Social Interaction: The Ethics of Stealth Marketing." *Journal of Public Policy and Marketing* 27(1), 45–56.

Case: Manville Corporation Fiber Glass Group (A), 2009, HBS, 9-394-117.

Session 5: Price: Ethical Issues

Objective: To expose the participants to ethical issues in pricing.

Readings: Chapter 4: Ethical issues in distribution channels and pricing, *Ethical Marketing* by P. E. Murphy, G. R. Laczniak, N. R. Bowie, T. A. Klein, Pearson, 2004, 1e.

Case: Retail Promotional Pricing: When is a Sale Really a Sale? (A), 1992, HBS, 9-591-111.

Session 6: Promotion: Ethical Issues

Objective: To expose the participants to ethical issues in promotion.

Readings:

• Chapter 5: Ethics in advertising and on the Internet, *Ethical Marketing* by P. E. Murphy, G. R. Laczniak, N. R. Bowie, T. A. Klein, Pearson, 2004, 1e.

• Chapter 6: Personal Selling Ethics, *Ethical Marketing* by P. E. Murphy, G. R. Laczniak, N. R. Bowie, T. A. Klein, Pearson, 2004, 1e.

Case: American Apparel: Unwrapping Ethics, 2012, Ivey, W12134.

Session 7: Place: Ethical Issues

Objective: To expose the participants to ethical issues in distribution.

Readings: Chapter 4: Ethical issues in distribution channels and pricing, *Ethical Marketing* by P. E. Murphy, G. R. Laczniak, N. R. Bowie, T. A. Klein, Pearson, 2004, 1e.

Case: Atlas-Copco (A): Gaining and Building Distribution Channels, 1993, HBS, 9-588-004.

Module III: Ethical Issues with Respect to Marketing Research and International Marketing

Module Objective

The objective of this module is to expose the participants toward the ethical issues with respect to marketing research and international marketing.

Session 8: Marketing Research: Ethical Issues

Objective: To expose the participants to ethical issues in marketing research.

Readings: Chapter 2: Ethics in researching and segmenting markets, *Ethical Marketing* by P. E. Murphy, G. R. Laczniak, N. R. Bowie, T. A. Klein, Pearson, 2004, 1e.

Case: Avalon Information Services, Inc., 1996, HBS, 9-395-036.

Session 9: International Marketing: Ethical Issues

Objective: To expose the participants to ethical issues in international marketing.

Readings: Ethics and international marketing: research background and challenges by M. Carrigan, S. Marinova, I. Szmigin, 2005, *International Marketing Review*: Volume 22, Issue 5, pp. 481–493.

Case: GlaxoSmithKline in China (A), 2013, HBS, 9-514-049.

Module IV: Implementation of Marketing Ethics at Organizational Level

Module Objective

The objective of this module is to sensitize the participants toward implementation and audit of marketing ethics at organizational level.

Session 10: Implementation and Audit at Organizational Level

Objective: To sensitize the participants toward organization-wide marketing ethics implementation and audit.

Readings: Chapter 7: Implementing and auditing ethical marketing, *Ethical Marketing* by P. E. Murphy, G. R. Laczniak, N. R. Bowie, T. A. Klein, Pearson, 2004, 1e.

Case: NIL

Additional Reading(s)

- *Ethical Decision Making in Marketing* by L. B. Chonko, SAGE Publications, 1995.
- *Ethics in Marketing* by S. Horowitz, Jaico Publishing House, 2005.
- *Ethical Marketing: Perspectives and Applications* by K. Suresh (edited), The ICFAI Unversity Press, 2005, 1e.

- *Ethics and the Conduct of Business* (Chapter 10: Marketing, Advertising, and Product Safety) by J. R. Boatright and B. P. Patra, Pearson Education, 2011, 6e.
- *Marketing Ethics: An International Perspective* by B. B. Schlegelmilch, International Thomson Business Press, 1998, 1e.
- *Marketing Ethics* (Series—Foundations of Business Ethics) by G. G. Brenkert, John Wiley and Sons, 2008.

CHAPTER 7

Teaching Ethics in Business: Experience at a University in India

Piya Mukherjee

Director, Vivekanand Education Society's Leadership Academy and Research Centre (VESLARC), India

Background

India is a vibrant, growing economy, considered one of the fastest grow-ing economies and one of the most stable democracies. In a 2012 survey conducted by the United Nations Conference on Trade and Development (UNCTAD), India replaced the United States as the second-most-im-portant foreign direct investment (FDI) destination for transnational corporations. With an estimated annual growth rate of 7.3 percent, and a middle class that will touch more than 547 million individuals (as esti-mated by McKinsey and Company), India is a very attractive destination for products, investment, and services.

Yet, continued growth seems to be stymied by growing corruption. As of 2016, India is ranked 76 out of 168 countries on the Corruption Perception Index, by the Berlin-based Transparency International. Bribery is often described as the bane for investors and entrepreneurs, both domestic and from overseas. The New York–based Ethisphere Insti-tute ranked 131 companies as Ethics Honorees in 2016. Exactly three of these companies were Indian, and two of these three companies belonged to the same group of companies. These are: Tata Steel Limited, Tata Power

Company Limited, and Wipro Limited. A report[1] revealed that *in a span of just the preceding 12 months*, the country had lost over Rs. 36,400 crore due to corruption.

Clearly, there was need for teaching Ethics. A quick look at the business schools and their syllabi reveals the following: First, some business schools include a discussion of Ethics in their syllabus while others do not. This means, many students have not been consciously sensitized to and trained in Ethics. This could affect the consciousness of decision-makers about the ethical impacts of their decisions. Second, business schools offer Ethics as an elective or a core course. When it is offered as an elective, course registrations tend to be low as students prefer functional subjects. When it is offered as a compulsory course—usually in the final semester of the two-year course having four semesters—student motivation to attend classes and learn is low as the term coincides with placements and the course revisits functional subjects already covered (which is wearisome). Third, faculty members teaching the subject struggle to teach it effectively partly due to inadequate training in the subject,[2] because they are not convinced of its relevance,[3] because the syllabi are not updated or because faculty have limited discretion in changing the syllabus/pedagogy. Some assign group projects on various topics across the entire semester, others adopt the chalk-and-talk approach, and yet others introduce case studies whose (foreign) context is often far removed from Indian realities.

This chapter describes the experience of teaching the course "Ethics in Business" in a University of India during the period 1997 to 2015.

---

[1] Source: http://ey.com/Publication/vwLUAssets/Bribery_and_corruption:_ground_reality_in India/$FILE/EY-FIDS-Bribery-and-corruption-ground-reality-in-India.pdf. Accessed on March 10, 2017.

[2] For instance, in some colleges, the faculty for Human Resource Management were cajoled into completing the syllabus, weeks or days before the completion of the semester.

[3] During informal conversations, some of them said, "How do we ask the students to be ethical, knowing that there are systemic issues?" Third, even when the faculty is willing to teach the course, there are systemic constraints.

Interventions

The Learning Objectives of the Ethics in Business course (which was taught for 18 years and has recently been dropped), as defined by the university are: (a) To have an in-depth knowledge of issues concerning morals, values, ideologies, and ethics in personal, professional, and business lives; (b) to prepare the budding managers and entrepreneurs to develop themselves into better corporate citizens; (c) to imbibe into students the importance of fair transactions, ethical conduct, and conscientious decision-making; (d) to expect an integrity-driven workplace scenario for students; (e) to ensure sustainability as a compulsive tool of driving organizational vision and mission; an (f) to have a balance between the theoretical and practical aspects of ethics in general and ethics in business in particular.

The class comprised 60 students, with about 45 boys. Most were 22- to 24-year-olds, largely "freshers" straight out of college. For them, the two-year MBA course was a passport to a high/higher-paying job. They were proficient in the use of computers. Though curious, they had poor reading habits, preferring dialogue to reading. While many wanted to do the right thing, this was tempered by cynicism. Some were very articulate in conveying their thoughts while many were uncomfortable expressing themselves in English. They were used to studying in the chalk-and-talk mode. To many, "Business Ethics" was an oxymoron: "How is it possible to be ethical while still being profitable in business?" they asked. "We can either make profits or be ethical—not both."

I was convinced the course had to be taught. The students had to know that being ethical was the right thing to do and how to do it. I felt the need to include a more practical, student-centric approach to ensure that students themselves discover the central learnings. Case studies, videos, role-plays, group discussions, introspective exercises, written journal work, newspaper read-outs, project work, and examples of leaders could be *more effective than mere theory*, in inspiring and sensitizing students to the importance of being ethical, provided they were contextually appropriate. Interviews with a few corporate leaders, videos, case studies, TED talks, and the Internet could be preferred to articles that needed reading. There would be a greater focus on discussion and debates over the inputs I shared.

I decided to expose the students to possibilities of "practical ethics" through several examples of companies that were doing well financially by doing good (in terms of governance and values). My role would be to share examples and facilitate self-discovery among the students. For example, I would point out the correlation of financial success with sound governance.

While the official course objectives did not change, I introduced new pedagogical interventions. The details of the design and conduct of the three interventions are summarized in Annexure 7.1. The next section describes the three interventions introduced into the course.

Intervention 1: Profit + Principles (P+P) Approach

While the central themes about Ethics would be covered, I wanted to include contemporary developments to make the course exciting to students. I was especially interested in introducing the practices of several Indian business organizations. The high-context culture of India has led to corporate approaches that are different from those in global multinational companies. For example, the use of "jugaad" or frugal innovation can be stretched to incorporate the approach of "Do whatever you need to do to reach the goal—just don't get caught!" It was with dismay that I watched such thinking grow over the years, wondering what role a faculty could play in introducing a different, more ethical approach.

I decided to cull out some common principles—which I called the "Profits with Principles" approach to business—that drew from Indian companies that have adopted more ethical approaches. These could become the guiding concepts for young managers. With time, the list of examples could include a more diverse, global set of companies and an examination of how they responded in different circumstances. I studied specific projects and initiatives of companies. This was not a part of the syllabus of the university, but I developed and implemented this in the course I taught there.

I started with a study of responsible management initiatives of well-known companies in India such as Godrej Agrovet, Holcim India, and so on. These initiatives were often triggered by a crisis/challenge. The company's response to the challenge seems to have stemmed from a desire to address the needs of people at the "bottom of the pyramid" while seeking alignment with their core competence. They were not charity oriented. They demonstrated a long-term, stakeholder-driven approach to add value. It appeared that a P+P approach was possible: Companies could attain financial success while being ethical in their relationship with stakeholders.

For the session, I did not prescribe any pre-reading. For the first 45 minutes of the session, I explained the concept of "Profits + Principles" using real-life examples of companies based in India and elsewhere. For the next 45 to 60 minutes, the students worked in groups to study an assigned company from the manufacturing or service sector and suggest ways in which the company could take a P+P approach at work. They were encouraged to use online resources to ensure that their suggestions are backed by hard financial and other data. These ideas were then presented to the rest of the class. In the next 45 to 60 minutes, the class was encouraged to identify winning ideas and ideas not practical or too challenging to implement. The discussion helped identify the conditions in which some ideas could work. In the last 15 minutes, students were then asked to write out their learnings from the process. Using real-life examples, the session helped illustrate the possibility for companies to make profits while following principles.

Students stated that they found the P+P concept very useful, inspiring, and refreshingly different. For some of them, this was the first exposure to the thought that being a good manager and a successful one were not mutually exclusive. Most importantly, this approach allowed students to use their creativity to straddle the gap between what is ideal and what is practicable. They found the group activity to be particularly useful in triggering the question: How do I do well while doing good for others? In future, this could be supplemented by (a) site visits to organizations that practice the P+P approach; (b) talks by senior executives from these companies that describe not just their success stories but their learnings from the challenges faced; and (c) assignments requiring in-depth research on how companies could leverage the P+P approach to create more impact to society.

Intervention 2: Student-Led "Action" Projects That Make a Difference

Typically, students often perceive a huge disconnect between their lives and the concepts espoused in textbooks. Projects requiring desk research are often introduced to supplement textbook learning. But they have limited learning or transformational value. Students typically download data from the Internet and create a patchwork of facts and figures. The question–answer session that follows a presentation of such a group project usually reveals the sheer pointlessness of such an exercise.

Hence, I introduced a live, activity-based transformative project. The objective of this assignment was to help the student put classroom theories into practice, learn about real challenges faced while undertaking any project, and gain the satisfaction of bringing about a change in the lives of people.

The concept of ethics and the "profits with principles" approach was explained in class. Students were given an overview of what they might want to define as their transformative task. Each group of students had to make a difference to an existing situation, either in the environment or in the lives of certain identified underprivileged sections of society. Here, the focus shifts from only writing about something to actually doing something useful, and then writing about it.

The project carried 20 percent of the overall marks for the course. The students were divided into groups of around five to six students each. Each group selected and drew a topic for their project from a prepared list of project topics. The projects were presented as an opportunity to make a positive difference to the underprivileged. Students were assigned a book related to their project theme. They had to read it and demonstrate their learning through a viva voce and a progress-assessment session. After this, they worked on the project.

The duration of the project was five weeks—long enough for students to read the related literature or book, plan their activity, implement the same, and write their learnings in the report. So, for example, one group might choose to first read up about social entrepreneurship, next, work with the staff and students of a school for the differently abled and help them market handmade products online, and finally, write their learnings in a report. Students spent the bulk of their time on the field. They were assessed for the project's impact and the sustainability of the change that the group made. This was seen by asking two simple questions: How many people are/were helped by your project? Will they continue to gain from what you have done after you have completed your work on the project?

These enabled students to move from "doing short-term good" to "making a lasting difference." So, for example, instead of organizing a sale of brownies and cookies made by underprivileged women linked to a nongovernmental organization (NGO), they would instead help the NGO win a contract to supply the same brownies and cookies to the canteens of several colleges. Each group video-recorded the work, submitted a 5,000-word, written report and some groups were asked to present their work to the class. Tables, flowcharts, and photographs are encouraged, where relevant. (Please see Annexure 7.2 for an indicative list of books and correlated projects.)

Initially, the idea of such a project met with resistance from the students—it was considered difficult. They balked at the idea of getting out of their comfort zone and actually doing a task. However, once they plunged into the project, many discovered that they were learning far more than conventional classroom inputs. Some benefits attributed to the project were: (a) greater awareness of their own personality; (b) soft skills and (c) application of a cross-functional perspective to deal with problems. For instance, students advising an NGO on better inventory management systems learnt supply-chain management, marketing, and pricing.

The opportunity to help a person or an organization in a sustainable way and the opportunity to personally interact with the people they helped seemed to be more impactful than an impersonal donation to a charitable cause. For example, a group of students who imparted basic financial literacy skills to blue-collar employees at their own college (e.g., sweepers/janitors, gardeners) and helped them open bank accounts felt good knowing that these people would directly gain from such an intervention even afterwards. The projects also offered scope for learning about the lives of people from vastly different socioeconomic strata and connecting with them. Students teaching moral values through folk-tales to a group of children at an orphanage gained an insight into the lives of the children and to "speak their language" so that the interaction was meaningful and respectful, not condescending.

On projects requiring some change in the existing systems at the field site (e.g., planting saplings, improving the garbage collection system, initiating a clean-up campaign, and better lighting to change the civic ambience) students needed to coordinate with and seek the cooperation from various relevant authorities.

Feedback over the past few years shows that some of these students went on to weaving social well-being-related activities with their mainstream work. The opportunity to read inspiring books was also appreciated in that it provided a glimpse of the lives of people who had transformed society. For example, students reading "The Last Lecture" or "Man's Search for Meaning" and then working with terminally ill children under the Make a Wish foundation began to reflect on questions like: How does my life make a difference? What am I contributing to others? A handful of students even find that their priorities and thinking have shifted for the better.

In future, perhaps a more formalized system of cross-functional assessment would help the students move out from a "silo view" of this subject, to a more holistic and realistic view.

Intervention 3: Everyday Heroes: How Ordinary People Can Do Extraordinary Things for the Greater Good

Contemporary electronic and press media have greater coverage of "bad news" than what is inspiring, pleasant, and reenergizing. This can lead to a belief that "the world is a bad place" or "the system is evil and corrupt." This could lead to a despondency reflected in "What can I alone do? It is better to conform" or, more dangerously "Since all seem to be opportunistic, let me also be the same." Alternatively, it could lead to a belief that one needs to be opportunistic through the working life but can do good things to society on retirement. In the absence of enough visible role models, most students would not believe that it is possible to combine doing good with doing well. Hence, it seemed to me that a faculty must work hard to bring the right examples to the classroom—the media was not and is not doing this job.

This intervention was a response to counter these beliefs/perceptions and show students how it is possible to make a difference for the better. I compiled and shared inputs on everyday heroes who are ordinary people who have positively impacted the lives of others. Some of them were well known while others were not. Some took up causes in addition to the work they otherwise do, others integrated their passions with their everyday work.

It aimed to provide students with much-needed inspiration drawn from the lives of those leaders, social activists, managers, professionals, and entrepreneurs who have chosen to use their work to make a difference to society, for the better. They epitomized "ethics in action," demonstrating how they overcame challenges to do the right thing at work and outside.

I used the print media and the Internet to cull out inputs on people from different walks of life to see what lessons could be offered to MBAs. Then, I defined a few questions, to be asked collectively to the class. Please see Annexure 7.3 for an indicative list of people covered. During the class, I spent about 20 to 30 minutes of a three-hour class discussing the life of a chosen person. I started by posing a challenging situation and asking the class how they would respond. Then I showed a video (or read from an article) that described how the chosen person responded. This was followed by a reflective discussion and summed up with a question on key learnings from the life of the chosen person, what inspired them or got them thinking. The focus was on promoting a *"can-do"* attitude.

Students said that they retained the learnings from these discussions far more than the discussions focused on abstract theory. They found it extremely inspiring to know that there were people doing what they thought was right and doing so without compromising on their other chosen pursuits. Furthermore, knowing about real-life instances of problem-solving enabled them to adopt a similar approach to problems in their own lives. Many of the students voluntarily sought further inputs about these "everyday heroes." Perhaps, most significantly, they learnt that one does not have to wait till one reaches a certain milestone (in terms of age, finances, or hierarchy at work) before becoming a change-agent—one could start in the here-and-now.

Talks by some of these "Everyday Heroes" could reinforce the "can-do" spirit. Furthermore, making the process student driven would lead to richer, more impactful discussions and learnings. Individual values are a necessary but not sufficient condition for corporate ethicality. Individuals who are equipped with a strong belief in the need to do the right thing, who have the desire to use creativity to overcome challenges, and most importantly, have faith in their abilities to transform organizations are better able to withstand challenges. However, this is not sufficient. The organizational systems and the cultural ethos must support ethical behavior.

Challenges and Outcomes

Across the three interventions, some of the common challenges experienced were as follows:

1. **Convincing students to view the projects as a learning experience.** In the initial phases of the project, students were hesitant to step out of their comfort zones and interact with the community in the Action Projects. Students not used to experiential learning may find themselves extremely uncomfortable when faced with the prospect of actually doing something that makes a difference, and further, being graded on the sustainable impact of that action. Repeated counselling and tapping into the latent desire of students to improve society can nudge them towards taking the projects seriously.

   For instance, students who read "The Last Lecture," by Randy Pausch and volunteer with Make A Wish foundation, might find themselves facing up to their own mortality—an uncomfortable space for a 20-something MBA student. The project holds the potential to sensitize the most cynical of students, as they work with young, terminally ill children.

2. **Finding alternatives to pre-reading.** Faculty members teaching in the university need to facilitate learning by adopting alternatives to pre-reading or to lecturing. Pre-reading is not expected at many educational institutions in India. So, students could be asked to read the concepts in class and immediately clarify their doubts. Classroom

discussions and debates would follow soon after. Second, some students could volunteer to read up on a certain segment for the upcoming class and then to explain the same to their classmates. This would invariably lead to a refreshing change of pace and "voice" in the classroom. Such participation could be encouraged by linking it to grades. Third, reading inputs could be modified into either equivalent, condensed notes, or substituted by short videos.

3. **Mobilizing stakeholder support for the projects.** While doing the projects, students need the following support from the stakeholders: (a) letters of permission from the administrative authorities to approach companies or NGOs for projects; (b) modest funding support to implement some of their suggestions at the project site, for example, buying and using "green" dust-bins, or installing eco-friendly lighting systems in colleges; (c) supportive actions by local civic bodies, for example, introducing zebra crossing or putting up street lights; (d) supportive changes in behaviors, for example, throwing garbage into bins, not elsewhere. It is not easy to institute these changes. In the short-term, it helps to demonstrate to the stakeholder how they might hope to gain value from the project of the students. In the long term, "Patience, persistence, and creativity" have to be the guiding words for faculty and students alike.

4. **Aligning syllabus with contemporary developments**. A subject like Business Ethics needs to promote a mind-set of asking questions such as: How are these topics in the syllabus relevant today? Are there newer contexts or exceptional situations that need to be studied? For example, traditional thinkers might believe in "ethics at the cost of profits" while newer thought leaders including late Dr. C. K. Prahalad might say, "profits and other goals in an ethical manner." Perhaps, this may gradually and organically emerge. More time may be required for such discussions. This could be a challenge in Universities, given the the constraints of the laid-down syllabus.

Outcomes

In their feedback about the course, students most frequently reported the following outcomes: (a) greater self awareness (strengths and weaknesses);

(b) greater understanding about ethics and ethical behavior; and (c) desire to use innovative thinking and creativity for win–win outcomes.

Conclusion

This chapter discussed three interventions made by the author to teach Ethics at a University. There is a need to teach Ethics in the Indian context. However, universities that include the subject have a prescribed syllabus that is not revised often enough. There is need to include contemporary approaches to better address the expectations of students and their attitudes towards Ethics. The content and approach to teaching the subject needs to be contextualized: They need to bring in live examples from society and from organizations that students are familiar with. They need to take into consideration the learning modes preferred by the students and promote high levels of interaction (debates, discussions) during the class without preaching. The course curriculum needs frequent review.

Additional Reading and References

1. Chakraborty, S.K. 1999. *Values and Ethics for Organisations: Theory and Practice*. Oxford University Press.
2. Krishna, R., and A. Tandan, 2002. *Business Ethics—The Indian Reality*. Vol. 14, Knowledge at Wharton.
3. Law of Karma. http://berkleycenter.georgetown.edu/essays/karma-hinduism; http://ramakrishna.org/activities/message/weekly_message41.htm; http://iskconeducationalservices.org/HoH/concepts/103.htm
4. Sims, R.R., and J. Brinkmann. 2003. Business Ethics Curriculum Design: Suggestions and Illustrations.
5. Gasparski, W. 2008. Responsible Management Education, Academic and Professional Press, Kozminski Business School.
6. Tilbury, D., and A. Ryan. 2011. "Re-Thinking Business Practice, Education and Learning in the Context of Sustainability." *Journal of Global Responsibility 2*, no. 2, pp. 137–150.
7. Parkes, C., and J. Blewitt. 2011. "Transdisciplinary Learning and Reflexivity in Responsible Management Education." *Journal of Global Responsibility 2*, no. 2, pp. 206–221.

8. Lavine, M., and C. Roussin. 2012. "Promoting Responsible Management Education Through a Semester-Long Academic Integrity Learning Project." *Journal of Management Education 36*, no. 3, pp. 428–455.

9. Verbos, A., J. Gladstone, and D. Kennedy. 2011. "Native American Values and Management Education: Envisioning an Inclusive Virtuous Circle." *Journal of Management Education 35*, no. 1, pp. 10–26.

10. Ray, S.K. 2007. Indian Economy, tax evasion, the black market— The Indian Economy, PHI Publisher; http://thehindu.com/opinion/ lead/black-money-the-hidden-wealth-of-nations/article8130657.ece

11. Collins, J. 2011. The Misguided Mix-up of Celebrity and Leadership, Conference Board Annual Report—Annual Feature Essay.

12. Rossouw, G.J. 2002. "Three Approaches to Teaching Business Ethics." *The Journal of Business Ethics 6*, no. 4, pp. 411–433.

13. Gandz, J., and N. Hayes. 1988. "Teaching Business Ethics." *Journal of Business Ethics 7*, no. 9, pp. 657–669.

14. Székely, F., and M. Knirsch. 2005. "Responsible Leadership and Corporate Social Responsibility: Metrics for Sustainable Performance." *European Management Journal 23*, no. 6, pp. 628–647.

15. Jackson, I.A., and J. Nelson. 2004. "Values Driven Performance: Seven Strategies for delivering Profits with Principles." *Ivey Business Journal 69*, no. 2, pp. 1–8.

Annexure 7.1

Table 7.1 Summary of the three interventions to promote responsible management

Teaching intervention	Intention + approach	Components of the process	Time allocated
1. Profits with Principles	Meant to enable students to use creativity to suggest P+P approaches for companies Group activity, with a small component of individual activity at the conclusion	• Explanation of concept • Sharing real-life examples • Assigning companies for discussion to groups of students • Group brainstorm • Group presentation and class discussion • Writing down learnings	Stand-alone segment of 3 hours
2. Meaningful Action Project	Meant to empower students to make a positive impact on their immediate environment, gain some insights into wider perspectives of decision-making, and test their ability to convert theory into practice Group activity, with a small component of individual activity, through a viva voce	• Assigning project themes and related reading, to groups • Book reading • Progress assessment and group viva voce • Field activity • Submission of written report, video recording of activity/activities • Presentations of selected projects	In class—3 hours for viva voce and 3 hours for selected presenta-tions; on the filed—15 to 20 hours of activity + report writing
3. People–Ethics–Values	Meant to inspire students with a "Yes, I can!" spirit, based on real-life examples One-to-many approach	• Description of an exist-ing challenging situation in the country; seeking solutions from students • Screening a video/reading out about a person who has faced that, or a simi-lar challenge • Study of how he or she responded to the situation, possible triggers of action, systemic supports, and hindrances	30 minutes in a session of 3 hours

		• Discussion of "what if" scenarios, reflection on own decision-making process, what a potential manager might learn from the person	

Annexure 7.2

Books, Related Learning, and Correlated Activity

Table 7.2 has an indicative list of the books assigned for learning, along with the themes of the project. To ensure that there is no "copy–paste" between two batches of students, and to have freshness of perspective, the books, and the project themes, change from year to year. Students are always welcome to suggest other topics too.

A question that might arise is: On what basis have these books been chosen? The single common thread running between them all is— their ability to have the student view life from a wider perspective. And, needless to add, these are books that I have personally found extremely inspiring. They do not belong to any one style of writing or genre, and span the thoughts of writers from India as well as other countries.

Table 7.2 A List of books suggested to students in preparation for serving the community through projects

No.	Book	Analysis	Field work
1.	*Old Path, White Clouds*—Thich Nhat Hanh	• Gist of the book • Key learnings for students • Convergence with Indian way of thought	Transformative work: Choose one process/event/situation in the immediate environment and improve or enhance it in a sustainable way. (e.g., Helping one's institute switch to more power-efficient lighting systems, initiating a system of collection of waste paper for sale to raise funds for underprivileged children, studying and changing the way in which garbage is collected on campus, to enable higher levels of hygiene and cleanliness.)

(Continued)

Table 7.2   (Continued)

No.	Book	Analysis	Field work
2.	*Katha Upanishad* (any publishing house)	• Gist of the book • Key learnings for students • Relevance in management	Learning + action: Create 3 moral science modules (of 30 minutes each) for primary and secondary school children and help them understand choices, consequences, and excellence. In the presence of the teachers, conduct the workshops.
3.	*An Autobiography of a Yogi*—Param-hansa Yogananda	• Key learnings for students • Rationality, faith, and belief	Transformative work: Choose one process/event/situation in the immediate environment and improve or enhance it in a sustainable way
4.	*The Kural*—Tiruvalluvar Translated by P. S. Sundaram	• Key learnings • Strategic lessons in resource management, leadership, administration	Design and implement: A half-day workshop for 100 students (junior college/undergraduate/postgraduate) on how they can use the Kural for a better life.
5	*To the Youth of India*—Swami Vivekananda	• Key learnings • Relevance in present-day life • What India can do for the world	Design and implement: A half-day intra-college seminar or workshop on nation-building through the learnings of Swami Vivekananda
6	*Discovering your Hidden Spiritual Resources*—Eknath Easwaran	• Key learnings • Relevance for young professionals • Correlation with personal lives	Service: Volunteer 60 man-hours (6 students * 10 hours each) at a local orphanage. Teach children—personal hygiene, teamwork, daily habits, civic sense, basic maths, one life skill
7	*The Road less Travelled*—M Scott Peck	• Key learnings • Relevance for young professionals	Service: Volunteer 60 man-hours (6 students * 10 hours each, 2 students at a time) at a local orphanage. Teach children—personal hygiene, teamwork, daily habits, civic sense, basic maths, one life skill
8	*The Power of Now*—Eckhart Tolle	• Key learnings • Personal action plan to change one area of life	Design and implement: A half-day workshop for first-year MBA students, on time and priority management, goal planning, and living in the present moment

9	*The Last Lecture* —Randy Pausch	• Key learnings • "What would I want to achieve if I were to die in a year's time?"	Action: Help 6 underprivileged people either find a sustainable solution to a persistent problem, **or,** join hands with Make A Difference/Make a Wish foundation and help fulfill the last wishes of 2 terminally ill children, **or,** create a blood donor's registry for the college (with at least 100 members and 20 members with rare blood groups) and organise a blood donation drive
10	*Man's Search for Meaning*—Viktor Frankl	• Key learnings • Correlation with personal and observed instances of challenges and their learnings	Action: Help 6 underprivileged people either find a sustainable solution to a persistent problem, **or,** join hands with Make A Difference/Make a Wish foundation and help fulfill the last wishes of 2 terminally ill children, **or,** create a blood donor's registry for the college (with at least 100 members, and 20 members with rare blood groups) and organize a blood donation drive
11	Wisdom Leadership-Dialogues and Reflections—Dr. S. K. Chakraborty	• Key learnings • Personal correlation with specific concepts	Knowledge: Interview 3 heads (CEOs) from the top 20 of the ET 500 (2014 list) of Indian companies. Then, invite one of them to the college, to address the students on leadership learnings

CEOs, chief executive officers; The Economic Times newspaper

Annexure 7.3

An Indicative List of People Discussed Under the People–Ethics–Values Intervention

(a) J. S. Parthibhan (a banker of Salem, who brings to his work a unique combination of creativity, efficiency, productivity, humility, and a desire to work toward social well-being)

(b) Kiran Bedi (Magsasay Award winner, former policewoman)

(c) Anuradha Koirala (founder of Maiti Nepal, has rescued over 18,000 girls from the flesh trade)

(d) Ramesh Sharma (India's only policeman to have won the Vriksha Mitra award for having helped plant over 2 lakh (2,00,000) trees in Damoh, Madhya Pradhesh, and has started a school for orphans and run-aways, at a railway platform in Chhatisgarh

(e) Subroto Bagchi (formerly with Mindtree Consulting, who follows and inspires others to follow principles of good governance)

(f) Baba Amte (the late social entrepreneur who created Anandvan, a self-reliant community for the ostracized lepers of Maharashtra)

(g) E. Sreedharan (a former beaureaucrat who has epitomized an efficient, corruption-free, and technologically advanced way of work at the Delhi Metro and the Konkan Railway projects, in an environment known for its chronic red-tapism)

(h) Anita Roddick (founder of Body Shop, known for connecting community to profitability)

(i) Erin Brokovich (who overcame the challenges of dyslexia, single parenting, and financial worries to successfully take on Pacific Gas and Electricity, over the leak of the highly toxic and carcinogenic Chromium 6 into the environment)

(j) Adi Godrej (business scion who chose not to enter into the cigarette industry in the early seventies, thereby rejecting the easy profits, choosing instead to focus on selling goods and services that enhance the quality of life of the common man in India).

(k) Mallika Jagad (of Taj Hotels, a banquet manager in her early twenties, who displayed calm courageousness, grit, and true leadership during the November 2008 terrorist attack at the Taj Hotel, Mumbai)

Other, men and women, campaigning for cleaner air, less noisy neighbourhoods, more trees and less hoardings on trees, safer roads, and lesser illegal constructions, and so on, are also part of this series.

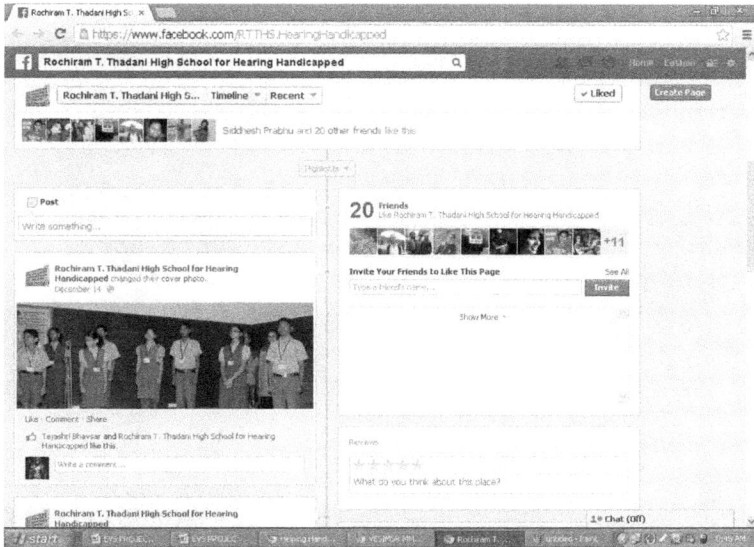

Figure 7.1 A screen shot of a Facebook page created by a group of MBA students, for the Rochiram Thadani School for the Hearing Handicapped, Chembur, Mumbai. The idea was to help create an e-platform to reach out to a wider group of stakeholders, specifically donors and those interested in marketing or purchasing products made by some of the students of this school

CHAPTER 8

Meeting the Unmet Needs of the Rural Poor—Applying the MOIP Framework in a Course on Rural Marketing

Ajith P

Formerly Assistant Professor, KIIT School of Rural Management, India

Background

Rural development has assumed global attention especially among the emerging nations like India, where majority of the population (about 69 percent) lives in rural areas. The present strategy of rural development in India mainly focuses on poverty alleviation, and aims to improve the quality of life through better livelihood opportunities and provision of basic amenities and infrastructure facilities through innovative programs of wage and self-employment. A recent McKinsey Global Institute (MGI) study talks about the need for India to move from the poverty line to an "empowerment line" paradigm According to MGI, the "empowerment line" is a new and more holistic measure of income deprivation. It is an estimate of the minimum economic cost for a household to fulfill eight basic needs, namely food, energy, housing, drinking water, sanitation, health care, education, and social security, which is sufficient to achieve a decent standard of living (rather than mere subsistence). The study reports that 35 percent of Indians are above the poverty line but below this empowerment line (Pande 2014). India can bring more than 90 percent of its people above the empowerment line in just a decade by implementing inclusive reforms to meet the eight basic needs.

Business can help address the basic needs of rural consumers by developing appropriate products/services and adapting their value propositions and market strategies. Given the roughly 850 million people living in villages across India, most companies recognize that they cannot afford to overlook these consumers. According to recent Nielsen estimates, consumption in rural areas is growing at 1.5 times the rate in urban areas, and today's $12 billion consumer goods market in rural India is expected to hit $100 billion by 2025 (Kapur et al. 2014).

Companies that have proved most successful in Indian rural markets have helped improve rural consumers' standard of living by creating jobs, building social infrastructure, or providing business opportunities. To foster these kinds of improvements, companies need to align their long-term interests with the rural community's development to gain its trust and commitment. This alignment builds synergistic relationships based on shared goals and aspirations. Corporations will have to reinvent themselves and be prepared for an exciting but long road ahead of them if they want to serve the rural markets.

Managers need to be prepared to identify the under-served needs of the rural community, develop appropriate products/services and develop marketing strategies to help rural people access and use these products/services. This chapter details the experience of trying to inculcate these competencies in a course on Rural Marketing at the KIIT School of Rural Management.

Institution

KIIT University has made a very conscious decision to start Kalinga Institute of Social Sciences (KISS) and the KIIT School of Rural Management (KSRM) to contribute to improving the quality of life in rural areas. The KISS promotes education and livelihoods among 17,000 tribal children, while KSRM trains students to provide managerial support to improve the quality of rural institutions. With a modest beginning in 1993, KIIT now boasts of 16 academic campuses housing 21 different schools in domains ranging from technology to management and from medicine to humanities. KIIT University had the unique distinction of being the youngest educational institution in the country to be declared a university (U/S 3 of the UGC Act, 1956). Academic programs of the KIIT University are approved by the Statutory Bodies of the Government of India, besides University Grants Commission (UGC). It is education coupled with empathy that makes KIIT stand out from the rest.

KIIT School of Rural Management

The KIIT School of Rural Management (KSRM), located in Bhubaneswar city, the capital of Odisha state of India, came into existence on November 20, 2006, in the premises of the KIIT University. KSRM has made rapid strides in promoting the rural management discipline as a specialized body of knowledge in the context of a developing country like India. The vision of the school is to use a knowledge-driven approach to become a leading global academic institution in the field of rural management. The mission of KSRM is to catalyze the process of sustainable and holistic rural development and minimize existing rural–urban divide. KSRM strives to achieve its mission through teaching, training, and research in the field of rural management and educating a new breed of professional rural managers having appropriate values and ethos to help rural organizations and institutions in professional management.

The Program on Rural Management

KSRM is a dedicated school for MBA (Rural Management) program under KIIT University. KSRM's mission is realized through generating, disseminating, and applying relevant knowledge innovatively to solve problems of rural sector. The MBA (Rural Management) prepares students for managerial positions in a wide variety of institutions working for the rural population. Each batch comprises 30 to 40 students who are graduates with an engineering, management, science, commerce, arts, social work, or agriculture background. Most students are between 20 and 23 years old, and belong to the middle-income group. A few students belonging to the tribes of Odisha avail free education as per the KIIT University policies. The profile of the last three batches is given in Annexure 8.1.

Students learn by listening to and interacting with faculty, peers, and also executives of various partner organizations where they do the field projects. They also learn experientially during the three field segments of 60 days each. Students expect quality education in the area of rural management and final placement in various organizations in the rural sector.

The program has two specific segments—Class Room Segment (CRS), spread over 55 weeks, and Field Segments (FS) of 33 weeks spread over four semesters. The field segment is divided into three components: (a) the Action Research Segment in Semester I, year one; (b) the Case Study Segment in Semester II in year one; (c) the Management Traineeship Segment (MTS) in Semester III in year two. To graduate, each student has to complete 92 Credits—56 Credits of Course work and 36 credits of Field Work.

In the field segments of the program, the students get opportunities to apply their classroom learning and sharpen their ability to solve problems in real-life rural situations. KSRM works closely with more than 250 partner organizations—including government agencies, various multinational and Indian corporate houses, international and national NGOs, and rural enterprises—to provide internship and also final placement to the graduating MBA (Rural Management) students. The program emphasizes the development of soft skills among the students. The institute's assessment center evaluates the soft skills of each student and develops a plan to prepare them for placements.

Responsible management is an integral part of the two-year full-time MBA—it is embedded in various compulsory and elective courses. The Rural Marketing course is an example of how responsible management is integrated into the program's curriculum. During the course on Rural Marketing, students expect a good understanding of the challenges in rural marketing and how to address the challenges with the help of concepts, frameworks, and best practices in the domain of marketing.

This case study illustrates the objective, methodology, and outcome of the Marketing Opportunity Identification Process (MOIP) module of the course on Rural Marketing.

Intervention

The Rural Marketing course is a compulsory course delivered during the third semester of the MBA program. Rural marketing is defined as the entrepreneurial and sustainable process of empowering rural consumers, communities, and organizations to enter into exchange relationships for value creation that will ensure well-being of all stakeholders and rural society at large (Paninchukunnath 2015). The broad objective of the Rural Marketing course is to build awareness about the various market exchanges possible with rural people who are one of the participants in the value-exchange process. The course highlights the opportunities available to fulfill the unmet needs and aspirations of rural consumers. Good competency to understand and solve the problems of rural consumers, households, and communities in creative and innovative ways is an outcome expected from the course.

The competencies for Sustainable rural marketing include the following: (1) the ability to understand rural consumers, community, and institutions—their culture and lifestyle; (2) the ability to identify basic needs and market to rural consumers, households, community, and institutions; and (3) the ability to enhance rural consumption by including the rural poor in the product development cycle (PDC) (Craig and Douglas 2011). "Inclusive marketing" looks at the rural poor as producers, suppliers, and consumers. Giving voice, visibility, and velocity to their creativity and knowledge is one of the key goals of inclusive marketing. The identification of critical needs of the poor, and the assessment of acceptability and affordability of new products is very critical for rural markets (Sheth and Sisodia 2011).

Keeping this in mind, the author introduced a module on identifying and meeting the unmet needs of the rural poor called Marketing Opportunity Identification Process (MOIP). It was embedded within the rural marketing strategy section of the course (see Figure 8.1). The MOIP project was designed to help inculcate (through field experience) the knowledge and skills for adopting an inclusive approach to new product development.

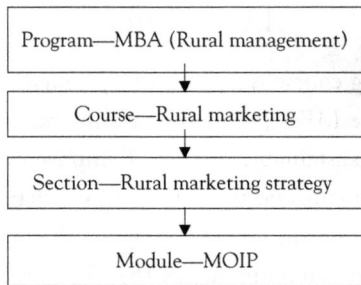

Figure 8.1 The embedding of MOIP module within the program

The MOIP Module: Design, Organization, and Execution

The MOIP framework was developed by the author to address (a) the lack of inclusive approaches to identifying opportunities in rural markets; (b) the lack of a comprehensive framework to capture critical elements of rural marketing opportunity; and (c) more fundamentally, to discover whether such opportunities exist in Indian rural markets. Facilitating the discovery of opportunity, however small and nascent, was the moral responsibility of any faculty member interested in holistic and sustainable rural development.

The MOIP framework helped students ask some strategic questions regarding the existing or latent opportunities in the rural markets of India. (Please see Annexure 8.2 for details). This had to be supplemented by a successful marketing strategy. Marketers had to ensure that customers were aware of the product and that the product was affordable, accessible and acceptable to them. The MOIP framework would help students develop new product ideas for rural markets and devise customer centric marketing strategies. The five key steps of using the MOIP framework is given in Annexure 8.3.

Organization of the MOIP Project

Organization of the MOIP field project. The students are divided into groups of four and each group is assigned one basic need to work on. Each group takes on the role of marketing professionals and thinks through all the key challenges and opportunities in designing a product to meet that specific need. They extract data from secondary sources and through interaction with practitioners operating in the same field.

At the end of the exercise, each group develops a product or service idea (sketches/prototypes of products or process flow for services) that could address the unmet basic need of rural poor in a sustainable way. Each team makes a presentation of their idea to the class—why they think there is an opportunity in the rural market, what are the challenges in the target market and how they can be overcome, why they think the target customers will adopt their product or service, why they think the marketing program is innovative and will be sustainable. If the groups have developed the prototype of tangible product or the process for service delivery, the same is also demonstrated in the class. Some examples of application of the MOIP framework to discover opportunities in meeting the needs of the poor are shared in Annexure 8.4.

Challenges and Outcomes of the MOIP Module

The main challenge in teaching this module is to make the students empathize with the rural poor. This is critical to motivate them to put in efforts to comprehend the rural poor. Empathy for the poor is critical for developing an in-depth understanding of the rural context. Motivating students to think through and apply the MOIP framework to the context can be time consuming. The faculty member needs to spend a good amount of time with each group to motivate them as well as to understand their thought process. If done in a workshop mode, the systematic instruction can take four to five hours.

The author has used the MIOP framework with three batches of MBA (Rural Management) program since 2013. In all the three batches, the response was almost the same. The reactions of the students was mixed: A few students took great interest and worked seriously on the project while the others found the project experience challenging. They struggled to identify innovative and sustainable solutions to the unmet basic needs of the rural poor. Only about 30 to 40 percent of the groups willingly made prototypes and exhibits to showcase the features of the product that could address the unmet rural needs. There was a resistance among some students to go to rural areas to engage with rural people to understand their needs and circumstances. Some teams tended to skip some parts of MOIP framework.

Some possible reasons for the resistance to the project include the students' lack of work experience, lack of exposure to rural context, lack of exposure to experiential learning (prior learning has emphasized rote learning or exam-oriented learning and not out-of-box thinking), aversion to risk/ambiguity, and lack of team skills. The low weight assigned for the MOIP exercise (10 to 15 percent of the rural marketing course evaluation) could also explain the level of involvement of students in the project.

The module potentially sensitizes the students to the various basic unmet needs of rural consumers, households, and communities and helps them to think deeply about the various unmet needs in rural areas. The application of the MOIP module demands information search and also holistic thinking on the part of students in order to identify the marketing opportunities available in rural India. Students are exposed to the challenges involved in developing an innovative and sustainable solution. The module potentially enhances the collaboration, creativity, and teamwork skills of all the students as the task is very challenging. The teams are constantly reminded by the author to search for innovative and sustainable solutions for the rural consumer's problems. This forces them to think out of the box.

Conclusion

Given the competitive environment, many companies are exploring rural markets. To empower the poor, they need to develop new products/services that address the unmet basic needs of the poor. They also need to develop suitable marketing strategies that enable the rural poor to access and use of these products/services. Sustainable rural marketing can be achieved only by developing three capabilities, namely (1) ability to understand the rural consumers, communities, and institutions—their culture and lifestyle; (2) ability to identify needs and market to rural consumers, households, communities, and institutions; and (3) ability to enhance rural consumption by including the rural poor in the PDC.

Keeping this in mind, the course on Rural Marketing was redesigned to include the MOIP module. The need for this framework arose from (a) the lack of inclusive approaches to opportunity-identification process in rural markets; (b) the lack of a comprehensive framework to capture critical elements of rural marketing opportunity; and (c) the need to establish whether opportunity actually exists in Indian rural markets. As part of the module, students undertook a project to identify unmet rural needs and develop a product prototype to meet that unmet need. Students found the project challenging. The instructor had to spend much time helping them to make sense of the project. Some groups of students put in the required effort to meet the project objectives while others resisted the project or struggled to complete its demanding requirements and come up with a product portfolio. Nevertheless, the project created awareness about the circumstances of the poor and the challenges in designing a product to serve their basic unmet needs.

Notes

McKinsey Global Institute. 2014. "From Poverty to Empowerment: India's Imperative for Jobs, Growth, and Effective Basic Services" available at file:///C:/Users/Ajith/Downloads/From_poverty_to_empowerment_Indias_imperative_for_jobs_growth_and_effective_basic_services_Full_report.pdf (accessed September 24, 2015).

World Population Data sheet. 2010. retrieved from http://prb.org/pdf10/10wpds_eng.pdf (accessed September 14, 2015).

References

Govindarajan, V. 2012. "Jugaad—A Model for Innovation" available at http://forbesindia.com/article/defining-debates-of-2011/vijay-govindarajan-jugaad-a-model-for-innovation/25512/1?id=25512andpg=1#ixzz1k6iaUBif— (accessed March 21, 2015).

Jha, M. 1988. "Rural Marketing: Some Conceptual Issues." *Economic and Political Weekly* 23, no. 9, pp. M8–M16.

Kapur, M., K.S. Dawar, and V.R. Ahuja. 2014. "Unlocking the Wealth in Rural Markets Mamta." available at https://hbr.org/2014/06/unlocking-the-wealth-in-rural-markets (accessed April 3, 2016).

Kotler, P. 2004. *Ten Deadly Marketing Sins: Signs and Solutions.* Hoboken, NJ: John Wiley and Sons.

Kotler, P., K.L. Keller, A. Koshy, and M. Jha. 2009. *Marketing Management: A South Asian Perspective.* 13th ed. New Delhi: Pearson.

Leonard, D., and J. F. Rayport. 1997. Spark Innovation Through Empathic Design. *Harvard Business Review*, Nov-Dec, pp. 103–13.

Manwani, H. 2013. "Leadership in a Vuca World" available at http://hul.co.in/Images/Harish-AGM-Speech-2013-Leadership-in-a-VUCA-World_tcm114-365167.pdf (accessed September 13, 2014).

Pande, V. 2014. "India: Not Quite Poor, Neither So Well Off" available at-http://articles.economictimes.indiatimes.com/2014-03-14/news/48222180_1_poverty-line-poverty-decline-eight-basic-needs (accessed April 12, 2016).

Paninchukunnath, A. 2010. "Rural Marketing in India and the 3P Framework." *SCMS Journal of Indian Management* 7, no. 1, pp. 54–67.

Paninchukunnath, A. 2012. Frugal Innovation, Design Principles and Indian Market. Conference proceedings, International Conference on "Marketing in Emerging Economies—An Agenda for the Next Decade" organized jointly by Punjab Technical University, Kapurthala and the Kenan-Flagler Business School, University of North Carolina (UNC), USA, at Amritsar (India).

Paninchukunnath, A. 2012. "B-Academic Scene: India to lead?" *SCMS Journal of Indian Management* 9, no. 2, pp. 5–12.

Paninchukunnath, A. 2013. Jugaad—The Indian Model of Frugal Innovation, Proceedings of the 2013 Annual Conference of the Emerging Markets Conference Board, Published by Nelson Mandela Metropolitan University Business School, ISBN 978-0-620-57660-4, pp. 151–163.

Paninchukunnath, A. 2013. "Value Proposition of Modern Management Education and India's Role." *Pacific Business Review International* 6, no. 4, pp. 15–24.

Paninchukunnath, A. 2015. "Rural to International: Blueprint for Marketing." *SCMS Journal of Indian Management* 12, no. 2, pp. 5–16.

Paninchukunnath, A., and A. Goyal. 2016. "Jugaad Innovation in Indian Rural Marketing: Meaning and Role." *SCMS Journal of Indian Management* 12, no. 4, pp. 5–18.

Prahalad, C. K. 2012. "Bottom of the Pyramid as a Source of Breakthrough Innovations." *Journal of Product Innovation Management* 29, no. 1, pp. 6–12.

Sheth, J., R. Sisodia. 2011. *The 4 A's of Marketing: Creating Value for Customer, Company and Society*. New York, NY: Routledge.

Singh, R., V. Gupta, and A. Mondal. 2012. "Jugaad—From 'Making Do' and 'Quick Fix' to an Innovative, Sustainable and Low-Cost Survival Strategy at the Bottom of the Pyramid." *International Journal of Rural Management* 8, nos. 1 and 2, pp. 87–105.

Subrahmanyan, S., and J. Tomas Gomez-Arias. 2008. "Integrated Approach to Understanding Consumer Behavior at Bottom of Pyramid." *Journal of Consumer Marketing* 25, no. 7, pp. 402–12.

Vaswani, L.K., R. Aithal, D. Pradhan, and G. Sridhar. 2005. "Rural Marketing in the Development Paradigm." *International Journal of Rural Management* 1, no. 2.

Velayudhan, S.K. 2011. *Rural Marketing, 2e*. New Delhi, India: Response Books.

Annexure 8.1

The profile of the incoming students from three batches: 2013–2015, 2014–16, and 2015–2017

Characteristics	Year			Characteristics	Year		
	2013	2014	2015		2013	2014	2015
Gender				**Graduation**			
Male	29	22	22	Bachelor of Business Administration	15	14	10
Female	7	12	6	Bachelor of Engineering	7	9	5
Home State				Bachelor of Commerce	6	8	4
Madhya Pradesh	1	1	0	Bachelor of Arts	3	1	3
Kerala	1	0	0	Bachelor of Computer Applications	2	1	0
Rajasthan	1	0	1	Bachelor of Science	2	1	5
Delhi	1	1	0	Bachelor of Social Work	1	0	1
Gujarat	2	0	0	**Work Experience**			
Jharkhand	3	11	4	Nil	26	27	20
W. Bengal	3	6	3	Less than 6 months	1	2	4
Uttar Pradesh	4	2	1	6 to 12 months	2	4	2
Bihar	8	4	2	13 to 24 months	5	1	2
Odisha	12	7	13	25 to 36 months	2	0	0
Maharashtra	0	1	2				
Himachal Pradesh	0	1	0				
Andhra Pradesh	0	0	1				
Tripura	0	0	1				

Annexure 8.2

Elements of the MOIP Framework

Part 1: Context of the opportunity—Under this section, the students are expected to clearly define the context or the target market. For the rural marketing course, the context is rural markets.

Part 2: The name of the organization and field of activity (sector/ industry)—Under this section, the students have to write the name of the organization and also the sector and industry to which they belong.

Part 3: Core competency—Under this section, the students are expected to clearly mention the core competency of the organization.

Part 4: Problems in rural area—Under this section, the students are expected to bring out all the problems of rural consumers/household/ community in the field of the activity of the firm. Against each problem, students have to rank the age group affected the most (children, youth, adults, or elderly) using a five-point scale with five representing "High" and one representing "Low."

Part 5: Challenges for marketing firm—Under this section, the students have to identify the challenges that the organization may face while trying to solve the problem and classify them as—high, moderate, or low. The challenges in all four areas, namely Context (Physical), Customer (Consumer Behavior), Competitors, and Need for Complementary products, have to be addressed. In case of context, the focus is on the physical infrastructure. Under Customer, the cultural, social, personal, and psychological challenges have to be discussed. Under Competitors, both direct and indirect competition has to be discussed. In case of Complementary Products, students have to mention whether it is needed and exactly what are needed.

Part 6: Stakeholders of the firm—In this section, the students have to identify the stakeholders of the firm and group them into primary, secondary, and tertiary.

Part 7: Marketing opportunity for firm (MO)—Under this section, the students have to mention whether in the specified rural area with the problems and challenges, is there an opportunity for the firm to intervene and offer a solution to address one or more problems in the area of its activity. The opportunity has to be identified from the temporal dimension as current opportunity (immediate), near future (within six months), or future (more than six months).

Part 8: Firm's solution (P/S—MO) to address the problem—In this section, the students have to clearly describe the solution and mention it under any one of the three categories, namely, similar to existing, superior to existing, or innovative. The product becomes similar to existing if an equivalent product is already adopted by the target segment. If the product has one or more superior features compared to the product already in use by the target segment, it can be mentioned under superior to existing. The product of the firm is innovative only if it is a totally new solution for the target segment.

Part 9: Profile of target segment (TS)—Under this section, the students have to describe the profile of the potential customer who will benefit most with the firm's solution (primary target segment). They should also describe the profile of the second most important group that may adopt the solution offered by the firm (secondary target segment).

Part 10: Customer value proposition (CVP)—In this section, the students have to describe the key benefits of market offering. They should explain how their product is different or superior to the existing products. For all the benefits and superiority claimed, sufficient proof must be provided so that the potential customers will get convinced.

Part 11: Check the 4As—Under this section, the students have to check the Acceptability, Affordability, Awareness, and Accessibility of the firm's solution by the primary target segment. This part of the framework will help the student to decide whether the firm's solution has any chance of winning in the market or whether it is a true opportunity. If all the 4As are found to be "high," the chance of success is very high. If all the 4As are found to be "low," there is a big risk in introducing the solution in the target market. A mix of "high" and "moderate" among the 4As may also have a chance of success when the As with "moderate" rating is taken special care of during and after the introduction of the solution. The 4As as a diagnostic tool was proposed by Sheth and Sisodia (2011). According to Professor Jagdish Sheth, the more customer-oriented 4As model is to be employed before undertaking to set the 4Ps. This model is built around the notion that the customer is the dominant actor in most markets. The 4As of marketing identifies four roles of customers to which marketers must respond if they are to be successful. Four As model is organized around the values that matter most to customers: Acceptability, Affordability, Accessibility, and Awareness. Taken together, these attributes are called the "4As." The 4As model is derived from a customer-value perspective based on the four distinct roles that customers play in the market. For a marketing campaign to succeed, it must achieve high marks on all four As, using a blend of marketing and nonmarketing resources.

Annexure 8.3

The Five Key Steps in Using MOIP Framework

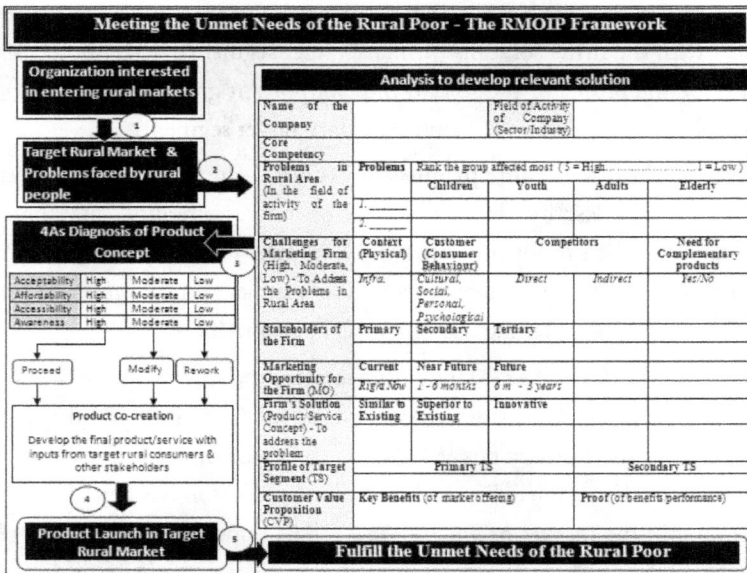

Annexure 8.4

Five Steps in the MOIP Framework

Context of opportunity—rural marketing opportunity					
Name of the company		**Field of activity of company (sector/ industry)**			
Core competency					
Problems in rural area (in the field of activity of the firm)	**Problems**	Rank the group affected most (5 = High....................1 = Low)			
		Children	Youth	Adults	Elderly
	1. _____				
	2. _____				
Challenges for marketing firm (High, Moderate, Low)—To Address the Problems in Rural Area	**Context (physical)**	**Customer (CB)**	**Competitors**		**Need for complementary products**
	Infra.	Cultural, social, personal, psychological	Direct	Indirect	Yes/no
Stakeholders of the firm	**Primary**	**Secondary**	**Tertiary**		
Marketing opportunity for firm (MO)	**Current**	**Near future**	**Future**		
	Right now	1 to 6 months	6 months to 3 years		
Firm's solution (P/S—market offering)—To address the problem	**Similar to existing**	**Superior to existing**	**Innovative**		
Profile of target segment (TS)	**Primary TS**			**Secondary TS**	
Customer value proposition (CVP)	**Key benefits** (of market offering)			**Proof** (of benefits/ performance)	
Check the 4As (high, moderate, or low)	**Acceptability**	**Affordability**	**Awareness**	**Accessibility**	

CHAPTER 9

Responsible Management Education: Summary

Background

This book emerged from the need for a detailed look at how some business schools in Asia are inculcating Responsible Management. It is based on (a) presentations at the pre-Forum Workshop on Teaching Responsible Management at the 6th PRME Asia Forum held at Goa, India, in 2015; (b) case studies submitted to the forum. The book provides a glimpse of why and how various business schools in Asia, especially India, are integrating Responsible Management into their curriculum. The business schools represented here include public and privately-owned institutions that are either part of universities or autonomous.

This chapter presents a summary of the main learnings under three sections: (a) why responsible management is gaining importance in Asia; (b) how business schools in Asia (especially India) are responding: and (c) some of the challenges faced in promoting Responsible Management Education in Asia. The chapter then concludes with some implications of these trends for the PRME.

Why Responsible Management Is Gaining Importance in Asia

Several developments in the business environment have triggered the demand for responsible management. First, participation in international fora such as the World Economic Forum has created awareness about the social and environmental risks facing society and their potential impact on the survival of business. There is a gradual recognition that these risks need to be factored into business decisions. Again, research has helped assess the impact of business on the natural environment. As a result, regulatory authorities in many advanced economies (and some emerging economies) have developed stricter norms for the conduct of business and continuously monitor compliance. Several Asian organizations have realized that their continued success and ability to access markets in the advanced economies (and some emerging economies) requires conforming to progressively stricter regulatory norms. Adopting responsible management practices helps them prepare for such a contingency.

Second, pressure from non-market stakeholders has forced business to conduct itself more responsibly. The following examples are illustrative:

(a) *The United Nations.* The United Nations has engaged business, governments and civil society in identifying critical social and environmental challenges and translating them into goals (such as the Millennium Development Goals) that need to be achieved in a specific time frame. These goals can only be achieved through collaboration between government, business, and civil society. The United Nations and its sister agencies therefore exhort business and business schools to help achieve these goals.

(b) *National governments.* The national governments of several countries in Asia have developed policies to encourage greater responsibility toward society and the natural environment. For instance, the Government of India has developed a more realistic (but still contentious) model to monetize the impact of business on the natural ecosystems and uses this to levy a substantial compensatory tax on companies that use natural resources. Increased scarcity of these natural resources would increase their valuation, in turn increasing the business costs of accessing them.

(c) *Vigilant social media, NGOs (national and international) and consumer organizations.* In India, consumer organizations have helped consumers become more aware about the unethical marketing practices adopted by some companies to market their products. They are also educating consumers about their rights. Individual consumers are progressively publicizing their grievances about service quality (of airline companies for instance) on the social media. International NGOs have taken up the rights of displaced communities and are using social media to seek greater accountability from large corporations who displace them. Companies have realized that such publicity could adversely affect their reputation and their ability to compete.

(d) *The public*. Public restiveness about poor governance and corruption among the political and economic institutions could also act as a trigger for responsible management practices. This is illustrated in Philippines, where two peaceful citizen-led revolutions against corrupt governments signaled that while economic growth is key, the people also want political and other institutions to be accountable.

As a result of these developments, there is a progressive acknowledgment that business needs to be more responsible toward society. Examples of well-known Asian companies that have adopted responsible management practices were discussed at the Workshop.

How Business Schools have Responded

Institutional Interventions

Institute-level interventions to inculcate responsible management in Asia appear to be driven by government directives and the vision and mission of the parent institution. It is interesting that students or corporate recruiters do not appear to be directly driving the demand for responsible management education in the sampled business schools, unlike in some of the more developed countries.[1]

The following examples are illustrative: The mission of the Colegio de San Juan de Letran Calamba is to promote total human development and help build a genuine community through an education that is Filipino, Dominican, and Christian in orientation. The University actively facilitates service to the community through immersion programmes and its community engagement programme. The Hang Seng Management College aims to be recognized for high quality education and for contributing positively to the community. Responsible management education

---

[1] Navarro, P. 2008. "The MBA Core Curricula of Top-Ranked US Business Schools: A Study in Failure?" *Academy of Management Learning & Education* 7, no. 1, pp. 108–23.

fits with this aim. The advisory of the Hong Kong Council for Accreditation of Academic and Vocational Qualifications (HKCAAVQ) to equip students with the competencies for sustainable development might have been an additional trigger. The KIIT University consciously started the Kalinga Institute of Social Sciences (KISS) and the KIIT School of Rural Management (KSRM) to contribute to improving the quality of life in rural areas. The KISS promotes free education among 17,000 tribal children, while KSRM trains students to provide managerial support to rural institutions.

Asian business schools have introduced some of the following administrative, curricular , co-curricular and/or extracurricular interventions for the purpose.

(a) *Responsible campus management policies and practices.* Some Universities, such as the Colegio de San Juan de Letran Calamba, Philippines, have set an example of responsible management through energy conservation programs, waste water management facilities, water treatment and re-use, waste segregation, avoidance of plastic on campus. The university also has a strongly developed community engagement programme and students are encouraged to be part of this. In Indira School of Business Studies, Pune, students collaborate with others to introduce sustainable waste management initiatives on campus.

(b) *Introduction of Centres to integrate responsible management into all academic activities.* Some business schools such as MDI Gurgaon, Hang Seng Management College, Hong Kong, and the Indira Group of Business Studies, Pune, India have set up Centres (for example, the Centre for Corporate Governance, the Centre for Corporate Sustainability and Innovation) to promote the integration of responsible management into their academic activities. In MDI Gurgaon, the faculty members are formally assigned to the Centre for Corporate Governance and trained in CSR or Sustainability. They offer courses, promote research, conduct executive development programmes and encourage student participation in competitive events on responsible management or sustainable development. In the Hang Seng Management College, conferences and seminars are opportunities for advocating sustainability to students, executives and faculty members. The Centre is also in the process of incorporating sustainability modules into several teaching programs of the college. In the Indira School of Business Studies, the Centre helped coordinate and review several initiatives to integrate responsible management practices in the curriculum.

(c) *Curricular interventions.* Some of the sampled business schools have introduced new programmes on responsible management. For example, the MDI Gurgaon has introduced executive development programmes and PhD programmes in the area of Corporate Governance and wellbeing. The KIIT University has introduced a postgraduate program on rural management to address the managerial needs of the institutions catering to the rural poor. The Colegio de San Juan de Letran Calamba offers a postgraduate program in Management (Engineering Management) that straddles two fields of knowledge—engineering and management. The program prepares academics and executives for teaching/practicing responsible engineering management.

All the sampled business schools appear to have introduced *new stand-alone courses (core or electives) within an existing discipline* on the theme of responsible management in their postgraduate programs. These include courses such as Contemporary Moral Issues, Ethics and Sustainability, Corporate Social Responsibility, Managing Sustainability, Ethics in Business, Ethics and CSR, Ethics and Society, Corporate Social Responsibility and Good Governance, and Marketing Ethics. There appear to be more courses on the subject of Ethics and Corporate Responsibility than on Sustainability or Sustainable Development in the sampled business schools.

The business schools have also included sessions or modules on responsible management (for example, sessions on Sustainable Development Goals, stakeholder management and on Giving Voice to Values) *into existing courses in their postgraduate programs.* These courses include Organization Behavior, Leadership and Emotional Intelligence, Rural Marketing, Business-to-Business Marketing, Sales and Distribution Management, Agricultural Entrepreneurship, and Transformational Leadership.

A few business schools like The Hang Seng Management College and IIM Indore have introduced modules on responsible management in their undergraduate programmes too. For instance, the Hang Seng Management College is introducing responsible consumption and production in the Operations Management module of its undergraduate programme on Supply Chain Management.

However, not all courses in the MBA curriculum have integrated responsible management. Integration of responsible management into functional courses is challenging partly because students do not accept such inclusions and partly because faculty members are not subject experts.

(d) *Co-curricular or Extra-curricular interventions.* Many business schools in the sample appear to have introduced extra-curricular activities such as community service and volunteer programs to inculcate an empathy for the poor. Students of the post graduate programme in management at IIM (Indore) participate in rural immersion programmes, school adoption programmes and internship programs that expose them to the circumstances of the poorer sections of the community. In MDI Gurgaon, students work as volunteers and contribute to community development. They raise funds for patients of life threatening diseases, educate children in rural schools, educate the poor on public health/disaster management and participate in the business school's CSR programme. In Indira School of Business Studies, students work as volunteers, help in tree-planting drives and "save fuel" demonstrations, and organize annual events on the theme of Sustainability. In the Colegio de San Juan de Letran Calamba, Philippines, students are encouraged to participate in the University's community extension service to serve the community. The University also has a 3-day social immersion program that is aligned with its mission.

In a few business schools/departments of management, service to the community is a co-curricular activity. Students serve the community in partial fulfillment of the requirements of a course. For instance, the course "Ethics in Business" at the University in Western India requires students to work in groups and make a small but positive difference to the community. For instance, some groups help NGOs improve their management practices so that they can better serve the poor.

Course-level interventions to Inculcate Responsible Management

Content. The case studies and Workshop discussions provide an indication of what is presently taught under the ambit of Responsible Management. Faculty members help students understand the concept of responsibility and why business must be responsible toward its stakeholders (including the poor). They help students identify visible and "invisible" stakeholders, create awareness about the perspectives of these stakeholders, and emphasize the need for synthesizing these perspectives to move in a common direction. They expose students to some of the ethical dilemmas managers face in responding to divergent stakeholder interests, build their capability to differentiate ethical from unethical actions and provide opportunities to practice ethical behavior. A few faculty members sensitize students to their own and others' values and how these can affect the attainment of an ethical, sustainable society. They address the skepticism of students about the practicality of ethical behavior by sharing several examples of companies and executives who have remained ethical. They also provide examples of ordinary people who have made a positive difference to society.

Pedagogy used. It appears that business school students in India lack managerial work experience. They are focussed on getting placed, have short attention spans, prefer learning through doing, and are sceptical about the practicability of responsible management. Business school students at Colegio de San Juan de Letran Calamba and Tsinghua University in China appear to have substantial managerial experience. They appreciate case based discussions. Those in the Tsinghua University's business school are also sceptical about the practicability of responsible management.

Faculty members from the sampled business schools use a variety of pedagogies in response (for example, short case studies, lecturettes, debates and small group experiential exercises). They help students relate personally to complex topics such as sustainability by using experiential exercises and activities. For instance, in the course "Ethics and Sustainability" in Bhutan, the instructor starts with the students' vision of a desired world and then gets them to reflect on what their responsibilities are to realize such a vision—what they (as citizens and managers) would be willing to give up or start doing to realize the vision. The course helps students relate to sustainability in a personal way. In the course "Marketing and Sustainability" offered at Xavier University, Bhubaneswar, students participate in debates to understand multiple perspectives.

Use of case studies. It appears that case studies are among the more preferred pedagogical tools in the classroom. Faculty members use case studies to achieve multiple objectives. One objective is to sensitize students to the importance of responsible management and the dilemmas faced in being responsible. In the course "Marketing Ethics" at the Indian Institute of Management, Indore, the instructors use Indian case studies to illustrate ethical and unethical marketing practices, explore the consequences thereof and suggest the importance of making ethical business decisions. In the course "Business Ethics and Corporate Responsibility" at Tsinghua University, faculty members used case studies to help students understand ethical challenges, realize the complexity and sensitivity of these issues, and use several theoretical frameworks to make business decisions that are ethical and financially prudent.

The second objective is to address student's scepticism about whether responsible management is practically feasible. In the course "Ethics in Business" at a University in Western India, the instructor shares several examples of Indian companies that are responsible and profitable. Students work in groups to study an assigned company from the manufacturing or service sector and suggest ways in which the company could be responsible and profitable. They begin to realize that companies can make profits while being responsible to their stakeholders. Case studies used in the course "Marketing and Sustainability" at Xavier University, Bhubaneswar, illustrate how executives in public and private companies implement responsible decisions in the face of opposition. Students begin to realize that responsible behavior is possible even in the Asian context. Faculty members suggest that being responsible to society provides business with tangible or intangible benefits. A few do bring in moral arguments for practising responsible management. However, in their experience moral arguments must be backed by business benefits too.

Lastly, case studies are used to help students think through the implementation of business decisions in a responsible manner. In the course "Agricultural Entrepreneurship" offered at the Indian Institute of Management, Ahmedabad, students use a stakeholder map to identify all stakeholders, explore their reactions to an entrepreneur's business decisions and plan a response that could be acceptable to all. In the marketing elective "Sales and Distribution" at the Xavier University, Bhubaneswar, students adopt the Giving Voice to Values approach to practice ethical responses in various business situations. However, the challenge is to get students to pre-read the case studies and supporting articles.

Use of projects. Some faculty members supplement classroom learning with project based learning. In the course "Ethics in Business" at a University in Western India, students do a community service project. They are exposed to the diverse stakeholder expectations while serving the community. The MOIP project in the course "Rural Marketing" at the KIIT School of Rural Management helped students develop product prototypes to meet the unmet needs of the poor. Students discovered the unmet needs of the rural poor and the challenges faced in accessing critical products.

However, in both the above examples, students who lack work experience struggle with the ambiguity and complexity of such projects. Some are reluctant to engage with such projects and need close guidance to make sense of these projects. However, students with work experience appear to appreciate such projects. For example, in the course on Environmental Technology Management at the Colegio de San Juan de Letran Calamba, students appreciate the opportunity to audit the environment management practices of their employers against accepted international standards. They learn as they move between practice and classroom learning, share observations with peers, reflect and propose improvements.

Students appreciate the opportunity to learn through doing, through self-discovery. In the course Marketing and Sustainability at Xavier University, Bhubaneswar, students learn about the perspectives of different stakeholders by conducting interviews of these stakeholders and doing preparatory research. Again, in the course Environmental Technology Management, at the Colegio de San Juan de Letran Calamba, the project promotes learning through self-discovery.

Outcomes. The MBA curriculum in the sampled business schools succeeds in making students aware about the need for responsible management. Students learn the challenges faced in reconciling the interests of business, society and the natural environment. They become aware of how business decisions can impact other stakeholders. However, the curriculum does not inculcate systemic, inter-disciplinary thinking and an empathy and compassion for people adversely impacted by business decisions. Project based learning could be useful even essential, to develop these competencies. However, the project design requires careful thought.

The frequently used community-service projects could inculcate some empathy for the poor: Direct, frequent and more personalized interaction with the poor can generate more positive attitudes towards the poor. Students who have participated in such projects report feeling good about making a positive difference to the poor. They report becoming more aware of themselves, of how blessed they are. However, partly due to the design of these projects, students often find it difficult to relate the learnings to the business context. As a result, it is likely that this empathy for the poor may not guide business decisions.

There is need to design new projects that (a) expose students to the complex, real challenges that business faces in addressing the concerns of society/natural environment and (b) offer opportunities to find sustainable solutions across functional or disciplinary boundaries.

Contextual Challenges in Inculcating Responsible Management

While there is acknowledgment that business schools should promote responsible management, there are several challenges in making this a reality. Fundamentally, the challenge is to introduce a different worldview of business—one that is centered on the wellbeing of people and the planet, not just on the (short-term) wellbeing of business.

Such a transformational change can happen when leaders of business schools acknowledge their responsibility to protect and promote the welfare of society, not just the welfare of corporate recruiters or the student body. Classroom discussions would then explore the implications of business decisions—both at functional and strategic levels—for the wellbeing of society, business and the natural environment. The workshop discussions and case studies highlight some of the operational challenges in transiting to a human and planet centered world view:

> *Infrequent revisions of syllabus and limited flexibility.* Faculty members working in public universities or whose business schools are affiliated to public universities indicate that the university syllabus is not very flexible and is not revised frequently enough. Those wishing to include contemporary developments or use different pedagogical approaches have a very small "window of opportunity." They need to find ways of including these new developments without compromising on the existing syllabus (however outdated some elements may be). This can reduce the effectiveness of the course in promoting responsible management.
>
> *Limited availability of appropriate learning materials.* There appears to be a strong preference for use of case studies to promote learning in classrooms. However, good case studies are in short supply. Faculty members expressed a preference for case studies and other learning materials that (a) are embedded in the Asian context; (b) reflect the complexity of business decisions including the perspectives of different stakeholders; (c) are suitable to the learning styles of Asian students. Some faculty members continue to use written cases based in foreign contexts while others have switched to videos to construct case studies that are rooted in the local context and provide data on stakeholders' reactions to the business decisions. A few faculty members expressed a need for pedagogies that instill an empathy for the poor.
>
> *Subject matter expertise.* Some faculty members expressed the need for greater subject-matter expertise in responsible management (especially on sustainability) to gain credibility among their students.

They expressed the need to understand the relationship between business, the natural system and the human system and to capture these in complex quantitative models such as climate change modeling. They felt that such models could improve the marketability of courses on responsible management in the post graduate programmes in management.

Functional mindsets. To better integrate responsible management across the curriculum, there is need to review the present discipline-based theoretical frameworks and develop/apply cross-disciplinary frameworks. This appears to be encouraged in some academic programmes, for example in the doctoral programmes in the Colegio de San Juan de Letran Calamba, Philippines. However, the functional boundaries appear to remain strong in many other business schools and are reinforced by students, recruiters, colleagues and administrators. As a result, the market for courses on sustainability or responsible management could be limited. It will be difficult to inculcate systemic thinking through the curriculum.

The Way Forward

It appears that responsible management is being introduced in the curriculum of Asian business schools. In post graduate programmes, responsible management is being inculcated through stand-alone courses and through modules within existing courses. However not all courses in the programme have integrated responsible management. As a result, students may be getting mixed messages from the programme. This could hamper the subsequent implementation of responsible management practices at the workplace.

To teach responsible management and sustainability, faculty members across functions need the following inputs: (a) greater knowledge about the relationship between the natural, economic and human systems; (b) learning materials (including case studies) that are context appropriate and capture the complexity of managing diverse stakeholders; (c) cross-functional perspectives for analyzing complex problems.

PRME Conferences/seminars could be useful fora for business school administrators to explore new perspectives about management education.

The PRME Chapters could serve as a useful platform for faculty members in the regions to (a) develop and share knowledge about teaching responsible management (b) jointly develop and use contextually relevant learning materials on responsible management and sustainable development. The PRME Working Groups can help researchers collaborate across disciplines to do research on responsible management, responsible management education and sustainable development.

Corporate members of the Global Compact Local Networks can support the above initiatives by (a) funding the initiatives of PRME Chapters and the Working Groups, (b) offering internships/live projects depicting the complexity of problems facing business today; (c) sharing data and their experiences of addressing the concerns of society and of business; and (d) providing feedback on the initiatives.

These initiatives would require a much stronger interaction between business and business schools in practitioner-initiated seminars and in scholarly conferences. They could also require much more interaction among business schools across regions. As more PRME Chapters and Working Groups take root across the world, there could be opportunities to share local and global practices and innovate.

About the Authors

Dr Ajith P was a Fellow of MDI, Gurgaon and a life member of All India Management Association. Before entering academics, he worked for fifteen years in industry. He started his professional career in 1995 with Lupin Ltd. and was also associated with Sanofi India Ltd., Cadila Healthcare Ltd (CHL) and BPL Medical. During his industry tenure, he worked in urban and rural contexts. His fields of special interest included Services Marketing, Sales and Distribution Management, Rural Marketing, Consumer Behavior, Retail Management, CRM, and Healthcare Marketing. He published articles in peer-reviewed journals and presented them in various national and international conferences.

As an academic, he worked at MG University (2002), ICFAI University (2005), Lancaster University (2009), Bharatiya Vidya Bhavan (2011), and IIM Rohtak (2011–12). Mentoring youth and nurturing their potential to take higher responsibilities was his passion. As an academic, he was very interested in the areas of business ethics, entrepreneurship, innovation, and leadership. Dr Ajith was a firm believer in Value-Based Management, Holistic Management Education, Experiential Learning, Mixed Method Research and Empowerment of BoP.

Dr Renu Bhargava pursues her passion for maximizing human potential. As a HR professional, she devoted a decade in creating end-to-end processes in areas of tackling retention, attrition, and other HR challenges in managing human asset, for an automated engineering robotic firm in Pune. Her desire to extend her learning to maximize human potential brought her out from the confines of a single organization to the arena of tackling management development programs and corporate consultancy. Realizing that growth and education share a mutually beneficial relationship saw her taking guest sessions in Industry Bodies and prominent educational institutions in Pune. The realization that a robust framework of technical education is indispensable for the growth of young leaders, she decided to work with the visionary team at Indira Group of Institutions, consolidating quality in the educational framework through achieving approval and accreditation from AICTE for her Institute.

She institutionalized Indira School of Business Studies as the first Autonomous Post Graduate Institution Approved by AICTE under the Indira Group. Her contribution to academics has been recognized by Industry and Academic Bodies in various forums. Currently she is the director at Indira School of Business Studies.

Mr Bijoy Guha an Electrical Engineer by profession began his career in Philips India and served with them for twenty-eight years in diverse cities and functions. He was seconded to the Cologne Plant (Philips Germany) in 1987 and on return took over the reins of the integrated Kalwa Light Factory, Bombay (1989)—the first Indian Manager. There-after, he headed the Professional Lighting Business in India. Finally, he was the India link in the international Philips Global Supply Chain—heading Corporate Purchasing in India, concurrently the Regional Manager (East), being located in Calcutta. He has actively worked with Prof Prahalad, Prof S Ghoshal, Prof Doyle, and other notables in the Philips Global restructuring initiative ("*Centurion*") in the early 1990s.

In 1998, he accepted the Tata's offer to start up a Joint Venture with Yazaki Corporation of Japan for Automotive Electrical and Electronic Distribution and Control Systems business. He moved to Pune and established Tata-Yazaki Autocomp to service Indian and Export require-ments of major car makers.

He retired from active service in 2003 and now serves Management Education as a "Visiting Professor" for Strategy and Operations for Post Graduate Programs. Mr Guha has mentored and incubated the "Sustain-ability" initiatives over the past eight to ten years particularly in the Indira School of Business Studies campus.

Dr Ruel V. Maningas is currently the Assistant Vice President for Academics and former Dean of the Graduate School and Professional Services of Colegio de San Juan de Letran-Calamba, Philippines. He obtained his Masters in Management and Doctor of Philosophy in Extension Education and Computer Science (as a government scholar) degrees from University of the Philippines Los Banos in 1995 and 2003, respectively. He is an alumnus of Colegio de San Juan de Letran Calamba Philippines, having earned his Bachelor of Arts major in Economics degree in 1987.

Dr Maningas is a strategist, professional lecturer, and capability building specialist in the fields of strategic management, knowledge management, research management, instructional materials development, extension and communication management, information systems, information economics, management economics, and business analytics. He had facilitated more than 100 trainings and seminars related to strategic planning, agricultural R&D management, information systems, and biosafety capacity building with more than 2,000 participants, both local and abroad. He is currently affiliated as part-time Professor at De La Salle University-Manila, Philippines, and University of Asia and the Pacific-Pasig City. He is also a consultant to the United Nations Environment Program (UNEP) providing technical assistance on building the country capacity towards participating in the Biosafety Clearing House (BCH).

Dr Maningas has prepared and presented technical papers in local research conventions and in international conferences held in the USA, Philippines, Japan, Thailand, Canada, Malaysia, and India. In 2007, his paper entitled "Providing Regional IT Advisory Services in Biosafety Education and Information: Experiences in Asia-Pacific" was awarded the "Best Technology Paper" during the 3rd International Conference on Agriculture and Environment Education. He was also invited by the publisher of Journal of Agricultural Science and Technology to be one of its technical reviewers.

Dr Maningas current interest is on the dynamics of educational institutions, the business sectors, and professionals vis-à-vis the ASEAN 2015 economic integration, responsible management education, and the seventeen Sustainable Development Goals (SDGs) of the United Nations. He has attended national and regional conferences with ASEAN 2015 as theme and is also negotiating with various higher education institutions in ASEAN member-countries towards partnership in enhancing the stakeholders' appreciation of ASEAN culture, educational landscape, and business and economic environment, to name a few.

Dr Maningas assumed the post of Executive Director of Council of Deans and Educators of Business-Region IV-A, Philipine and

President of Council of Deans of Graduate School in Region IV-A in AY 2014–2015. He was also the founding President of Entrepreneurship Educators' Association of the Philipppines-Southern Luzon, and a Regional Quality Assessement Team (RQAT) member of the Commission on Higher Education Region IV-A (CHEDRO-IVA) Philippines. He also assumed the position of Assistant Executive Director and Joint Secretary of the Asia-Pacific Association of Educators in Agriculture and Environment (APEAEN) Inc. from 2007 to 2012. He is also a certified ISO 9001 Internal Auditor, and a noted resource person in Outcomes-Based Education (OBE) and Innovative Teaching and Learning Strategies.

Prof. Melchor C. Morandarte is an entrepreneur as owner of Sir Mong's Food business and is currently the Program Chair of the Bachelor of Science in Entrepreneurship of E.T. Yuchengco College of Business (ETYCB) of Malayan Colleges Laguna (MCL). He already completed all his Academic Requirements leading to Doctor in Business Administration (DBA) at the Pamantasan ng Lungsod ng Maynila (PLM). He was conferred Associate Fellow in Business Education (AFBE) by the Philippine Academy of Professionals in Business Education (PAPBE). His contribution in the field so far is his international research presentation on the *Assessment on the Pivotal Role of the Philippine Entrepreneurship Education in the Development of Micro, Small, and Medium Enterprises (MSMEs) Sector in Osaka, Japan last 2015.*

At present, Mr Morandarte serves as evaluator and lecturer for University of the Philippines—Institute for Small Scale Industries (UP-ISSI), Diliman, Quezon City and a trustee of the Small Enterprise Research and Development Foundation (SERDEF), Diliman, Quezon City.

Piya Mukherjee has completed her Master of Management Studies (MMS) in Finance from Narsee Monjee Institute of Management Studies (NMIMS), Mumbai University. She has subsequently completed a Certificate course on "Management by Human Values and ethics—Indian insights," from the Management Centre for Human Values, Indian Institute of Management, Calcutta.

After working for five years at an investment bank, she has been teaching in the areas of Ethics and Human Values, and World Cultures, in

Mumbai, Singapore, and Dubai, at various business schools including Jamnalal Bajaj Institute of Management Studies, S.P. Jain Institute of Global Management, Somaiya Institute of Management, VES Institute of Management Studies and Research, and Narsee Monjee Institute of Management Studies.

She conducts training workshops for executives from India and other countries, at well-known organizations such as TCS, Reserve Bank of India, The Taj Hotels, Larsen & Toubro, Shipping Corporation of India, and the Government of Maharashtra, along with one-on-one coaching and train-the-trainer sessions.

She also contributes articles to several refereed national journals such as those published by the Indian Institute of Management, Calcutta and the Tata Institute of Social Sciences, and to business newspapers such as The Economic Times. She has published two case studies on Ethics which are available at the "Giving Voice to Values" website.

Presently, she is the Founder Director of Vivekanand Education Society's Leadership Academy and Research Centre (VESLARC), which is part of the 54-year group of educational institutes, Vivekanand Education Society. She is passionate about reading, nature, and holistic health.

Jayasankar Ramanathan is a faculty member in the area of Marketing at IIM Indore. His qualifications include BE from BITS Pilani and FPM from IIM Kozhikode. Prior to FPM, he was a member of R&D team at Cognizant Academy. His research and teaching interests are in the areas of marketing ethics and brand management. His research has been published in journals such as Journal of Business Ethics, Journal of Brand Management, Marketing Intelligence and Planning, Journal of Product and Brand Management, and Vikalpa.

Reynaldo R. Robles is a MM-EM (Engineering Management) graduate from Colegio de San Juan de Letran and has worked on companies that involve production and operations for over two decades. He is a Registered Electrical Engineer (REE) from Polytechnic University of the Philippines. He is currently working at Nippon Paint Philippines as Manufacturing Manager. He teaches in Graduate School, Engineering, Business Management and Accountancy.

Biswanath Swain is a faculty member at Indian Institute of Management (IIM) Indore, India in the area of Humanities and Social Sciences. He earned his PhD degree from Indian Institute of Technology (IIT) Kanpur, and MA and MPhil from University of Hyderabad. He has been qualified with UGC-NET for government lectureship in all the premier institutes and universities across India. He teaches courses such as Contemporary Moral Issues, Ethics and Society, Ethics in Business Management, Ethics and CSR, and Marketing Ethics at IIM Indore. His research primarily focusses on the issues in Ethics, Philosophy of Action, Corporate Social Responsibility, and Marketing Ethics. His research is published in journals including Journal of Business Ethics and he has also presented research papers at various international conferences held in the countries such as Australia, Germany, Japan, Malaysia, UK, and USA.

Ranjini Swamy is Professor of Organizational Behavior at Goa Institute of Management, Goa, India. She completed her Fellow Programme in Management from Indian Institute of Management, Ahmedabad, India in 1988.

Since then, she has taught courses in the area of Organizational Behavior and Human Resources Development at Xavier Institute of Management, Bhubaneswar and Goa Institute of Management, Goa. She has written cases and articles in the field of human behavior, management education, Ethics (the Giving Voice to Values approach), and Corporate Social Responsibility. She has published in the journals *Human Relations*, *Vikalpa*, and *Journal of Business Ethics Education* and contributed chapters in Principles for Responsible Management Education (PRME) publications and other books. She has also presented papers in the Academy of HRD Conference and the Eastern Academy of Management (International) Conference, besides national conferences. Some of her cases on Ethics are available on the Giving Voice to Values website at Babson College, USA. She enjoys reading, travelling, and experiencing different cultures.

Dr Shirley Yeung, an Institute of Environment Management and Assessment (IEMA) approved Sustainability (CSR) Practitioner, RABQSA, ISO9000 Principal Auditor, US, IRCA ISO 9000 Auditor, UK, AQIP

Assessor, US, HKCAAVQ Subject Specialist and Quality Management System (QMS) lead auditor of Hong Kong Quality Assurance Agency (HKQAA) of Hong Kong. In 2017, Dr Yeung was the Winner for the 2nd Global Young Leadership, Asia Week for her professional contributions to the community. She obtained Excellent Teaching Award, School of Decision Sciences, Hang Seng Magt College in the same year. In 2016 and 2017, Dr Yeung was the Chair of UNPRME Colloquium on Higher Education in Hong Kong. She was also the convener for the 1st Forum on Sustainable Development in Higher Education co-organized with UNESCO, APEID and the Chair of the 2nd International Conference on Supply Chain for Sustainability, Hong Kong, 2015. Dr Yeung was also invited by Harvard University, HPAIR to deliver a seminar on "Entrepreneurial Spirit and Sustainable Mindset" in 2015 and 2016. Dr Yeung also awarded "Pioneer Professor Certificate" from UN Flourish Prizes supported by UNPRME.

Index

This book is a publication in support of the United Nations Principles for Responsible Management Education (PRME), housed in the UN Global Compact Office. The mission of the PRME initiative is to inspire and champion responsible management education, research and thought leadership globally. Please visit www.unprme.org for more information.

The Principles for Responsible Management Education Book Collection is edited through the Center for Responsible Management Education (CRME), a global facilitator for responsible management education and for the individuals and organizations educating responsible managers. Please visit www.responsiblemanagement.net for more information.

—Oliver Laasch, University of Manchester, Collection Editor

- *Stop Teaching: Principles and Practices for Responsible Management Education* by Isabel Rimanoczy
- *Teaching Ethics Across the Management Curriculum: Principles and Applications, Volume II* by Kemi Ogunyemi
- *Dark Sides of Business and Higher Education Management, Volume I* by Agata Stachowicz-Stanusch and Gianluigi Mangia
- *Dark Sides of Business and Higher Education Management, Volume II* by Agata Stachowicz-Stanusch and Gianluigi Mangia
- *Teaching Ethics Across the Management Curriculum: Contributing to a Global Paradigm Shift, Volume III* by Kemi Ogunyemi
- *Managing for Responsibility: A Sourcebook for an Alternative Paradigm* by Radha R. Sharma, Merrill Csuri, and Kemi Ogunyemi
- *Educating Social Entrepreneurs: From Idea Generation to Business Plan Formulation, Volume I* by Paul Miesing and Maria Aggestam
- *Educating Social Entrepreneurs: From Business Plan Formulation to Implementation, Volume II* by Paul Miesing and Maria Aggestam

Announcing the Business Expert Press Digital Library

Concise e-books business students need for classroom and research

This book can also be purchased in an e-book collection by your library as

- a one-time purchase,
- that is owned forever,
- allows for simultaneous readers,
- has no restrictions on printing, and
- can be downloaded as PDFs from within the library community.

Our digital library collections are a great solution to beat the rising cost of textbooks. E-books can be loaded into their course management systems or onto students' e-book readers.
The **Business Expert Press** digital libraries are very affordable, with no obligation to buy in future years. For more information, please visit **www.businessexpertpress.com/librarians**. To set up a trial in the United States, please email **sales@businessexpertpress.com**.

www.ingramcontent.com/pod-product-compliance
Lightning Source LLC
Chambersburg PA
CBHW060529210326
41519CB00014B/3182